Emerging Trends In Computation

Matthew N. O. Sadiku, PhD, PE

Regents Professor Emeritus and IEEE Life Fellow

Prairie View A&M University

Prairie View, TX 77446

Email: sadiku@ieee.org

Web: www.matthew-sadiku.com

First Edition – 2026

ISBN: 979-8-2955-7208-1

DEDICATED TO MY FRIENDS:

Maxwell K. Ogundipe

Grace Ogundipe

Table of Contents

PREFACE

A problem is usually solved using one of three approaches: theoretical analysis, experiment, and numerical (computation). Today, computation is considered as an equal partner with theory and experiment. Computation (regarded as "computer experiments") provides a means of studying complex natural phenomena that would be too expensive or dangerous to study by direct experimentation. With the advent of large-scale computers, computational methods and analysis have become indispensable for simulating physical events and engineering systems. Computation has become an integral part of every sector of science and engineering, in addition to economic, social, and cultural aspects of our daily life. Today, various computational methods are used in all areas of technology, natural sciences, and social sciences.

Rapid advances in computing hardware and algorithms have changed our society. Many disciplines have undergone a computational turn in the past decades. The recent computational turn has produced subdisciplines such as computational humanities, computational sociology, computational economics, computational mechanics, computational fluid dynamics, computational science, computational electromagnetics, computational medicine, human computation, computational chemistry, computational finance, and many other computational schemes. They have been introduced for solving problems of all areas of knowledge. Many of these schemes have been developed into commercial software packages that make computation easy. These software tools are sufficiently user-friendly that one does not have to be a specialist to use them effectively.

This book explores emerging trends in computation. It is organized into three parts and 20 chapters that summarize various computation schemes.

Chapter 1 – Computational Engineering: This chapter provides an introduction to computational engineering. Computational engineering is a newly emerging multidisciplinary field that applies advanced computational techniques in solving complex engineering problems. It embraces engineering, science, applied mathematics, numerical analysis, and computer science. It applies techniques from these areas to solve complex scientific and engineering problems. Computational engineers can build several physical prototypes and test their performance early in the design process.

Chapter 2 – Computational Mechanics: This chapter provides an introduction to computational mechanics. Computational mechanics refers to the use of computational techniques to characterize, predict, and simulate physical phenomena and engineering systems governed by the principles of mechanics. It is an interdisciplinary research field with three major components: mechanics, mathematics, and computer science. The success of computational mechanics will be determined by its effectiveness in solving real-world problems of interest to society.

Chapter 3 – Computational Electromagnetics: This chapter provides an introduction to computational electromagnetics. The modern society we live in heavily depends on electromagnetic systems such as radio, television, radar, microwave ovens, mobile telephones, satellite communication systems, Internet, motors, generators, computers, transformers, and power networks. Computational electromagnetics deals with computational methods applied in solving electromagnetic problems. The main objective is to gain insight and understanding based on computer-implemented mathematical models of Maxwell's equations.

Chapter 4 – Computational Fluid Dynamics: This chapter presents an introduction to computational fluid dynamics. Computational fluid dynamics is an emerging branch of fluid (gas and liquid) mechanics that applies numerical techniques to solve problems that involve fluid flows. It is essentially based on the Navier-Stokes equations, which describe the motion of viscous fluid. It involves the numerical solutions of equations governing transport of mass, momentum, and energy in moving fluids.

Chapter 5 – Computational Nanotechnology: This chapter provides a primer on computational nanotechnology. Nanotechnology, the science of tiny things at the nanoscale, may be the new frontier in the transformation of every sector, from medicine to the food industry. It has led to significant innovations in the diverse areas of electronics, microcomputing, and biotechnology, as well as medicine, consumer supplies, aerospace, and energy production. Computational nanotechnology is the study, design, and optimization of nano-scale systems. It is emerging as a fundamental engineering analysis tool for the novel designs of nanodevices.

Chapter 6 – Computational Biology: This chapter gives an introduction on computational biology. It has been argued that computational thinking and computational methods are so crucial to understanding life that today all biology is regarded as computational biology. Computational biology is a branch of biology which is concerned with utilizing the capacities of computers to address problems of biological interest. It involves using computers to model biological problems and interpret data, especially problems in evolutionary and molecular biology.

Chapter 7 – Computational Physics: This chapter provides an introduction to computational physics. Several areas in physics have problems which cannot be treated exactly or analytically and must be solved numerically. Computational physics allows developing models of physical phenomena and understanding things at depths greater than possible otherwise. It enables learning physics with computers.

Chapter 8 – Computational Chemistry: This chapter provides an introduction to computational chemistry. Computational chemistry refers to using computers to model, simulate, and solve chemical problems. It has become a vital collaborator with experimental chemistry, whether it be physical chemistry, organic chemistry, biochemistry, medicinal chemistry, or chromatography. It is now an essential tool for chemists.

Chapter 9 – Computational Science: This chapter provides an introduction to computational science. Computational science refers to the application of computer simulation to solve problems in various scientific disciplines. A computational scientist is usually a scientist, an engineer or an applied mathematician who is skilled in scientific computing, programming languages, operating systems, visualization software, and parallel computing.

Chapter 10 – Computational Mathematics: This chapter is a primer on computational mathematics. Mathematics may be regarded as the manipulation of algebra which allows a solution to be found to a given problem. It permeates nearly all facets of life and is a necessary prerequisite for the vast majority of modern technologies. Computational mathematics is concerned with the study of algorithms (or numerical methods) for the solution of computational problems in science, engineering, economics, finance, and other fields. The goal of computational mathematics is to develop algorithms that solve mathematical problems computationally (i.e. using computers). Training in computational mathematics is essential for future careers in research and development in academia, national laboratories, or in industry.

Chapter 11 – Computational Social Science: The purpose of this chapter is to provide an introduction to computational social science. Computational social science can span all the five traditional social science disciplines: psychology, anthropology, economics, political science, and sociology. It is a multidisciplinary field that includes computational economics, computational sociology, distributed algorithms, statistics, machine learning, data mining, and several substantive social science fields, including sociology, economics, psychology, political science, and marketing. Computational social scientists develop tools that enable studying how humans think, feel, or behave in social situations (psychology), relate to each other (sociology), govern themselves (political science), handle wealth (socioeconomics), and create culture (anthropology).

Chapter 12 – Computational Art: This chapter provides a primer on computational art. Art is an open set of ways of acting inventively in culture. Computational art is the study and simulation of natural human creative behavior, by means of computer programs. It is a unique digital media program, training the next generation of highly skilled and motivated digital artists. Students in computational art are developed for an artistic practice that is conceptually provocative, technically innovative, and aesthetically engaging.

Chapter 13 – Computational Intelligence: This chapter provides an introduction to computational intelligence. Computational intelligence refers to recreating human-like intelligence in a computing machine. It consists of a set of computing systems with the ability to learn and deal with new situations such that the systems are perceived to have some attributes of intelligence. It uses various techniques such as artificial neural network, evolutionary computation, fuzzy system, support vector machine, deep learning, swarm intelligence, and hybrid methods.

Chapter 14 – Computational Statistics: This chapter provides an introduction to computational statistics. Computational statistics (or statistical computing) is a branch of computational science that is focused on statistics. It is essentially what statisticians do with the computer. It is concerned with efficient methods of obtaining numerical solutions to statistically formulated problems. It helps in the numerical solution of statistical problems.

Chapter 15 – Computational Economics: This chapter introduces readers to computational economics. The recent advances in modeling tools have greatly expanded the possibility set for economists. Computational economics is a marriage between computer science and traditional economics. It solves problems that are difficult to study without the use of computers. The new directions in supercomputing are beneficial to computational economics, which is crucial to the security and welfare of any nation.

Chapter 16 – Computational Finance: This chapter serves as an introduction to computational finance. Financial institutions and financial markets became increasingly dependent on computers and their productivity has improved steadily by the use of computers to manage databases and process transactions. A newly emerging field that combines mathematics, economics, and computation has become known as computational finance. While traditional finance deals with actually making transactions that range from stock trades to corporate acquisitions, computational finance is more concerned with algorithms, modeling, and the computer software that powers most of the modern financial world.

Chapter 17 – Computational Humanities: This chapter provides an introduction to computational humanities. The humanities cover what we commonly call the liberal arts: art, literature, history, anthropology, philosophy, music, media studies, archaeology, geography, and language studies. Computational humanities is at the intersection of computing technologies and the disciplines of the humanities. Computational tools supporting textual search, large database analysis, data mining, network mapping, and natural language processing are employed by the humanities researcher.

Chapter 18 – Computational Sociology: This chapter provides an introduction to computational sociology. Sociology is the study of the fundamental laws of social relations, institutions, organizations, etc. It deals with explaining and predicting social behavior. Computational sociology is an emerging area in sociology that applies computational tools to solve and analyze social problems. It involves using computing techniques, such as computer simulation and agent-based modeling, to analyze social phenomena and be able to understand, explain, and predict social behavior.

Chapter 19 – Computational Linguistics: This chapter is a primer on computational linguistics. Everywhere, every day, everybody uses language. There is no human society which does not employ a language. Linguistics is concerned with rules that are followed by languages as a system. Computational linguistics is based on the idea that machines can be computed to understand, learn, or output languages. It is concerned with the computational description of rules that languages follow.

Chapter 20 – Computational Medicine: This chapter provides an introduction to computational medicine. Computational medicine is a fast-growing method of using computer models to investigate how disease develops. It will provide a quantitative approach to our understanding, detecting, and treating diseases. Since biological systems are inherently complex, computational models are needed to understand their function in health and disease. Computational tools are now in the hands of doctors who treat patients with all kinds of illnesses. They should be multilingual and user-friendly so that they can be accessed by experts in different nations.

This book is a comprehensive text on the emerging trends in computation. It provides an overview of each emerging computational trend in a way that beginners can understand. It is a must-read for those interested in computation and its future.

I am grateful for the support of Dr. Annamalia Annamalai, the department head of the Department of Electrical and Computer Engineering, and Dr. Pamela Obiomon, the dean of the College of Engineering at Prairie View A&M University, Prairie View, Texas. Special thanks are due to my wife Dr. Janet Sadiku for helping in various ways.

M. N. O. Sadiku, Westlake, FL

ABOUT THE AUTHOR

Matthew N. O. Sadiku received his B. Sc. degree in 1978 from Ahmadu Bello University, Zaria, Nigeria and his M.Sc. and Ph.D. degrees from Tennessee Technological University, Cookeville, TN in 1982 and 1984 respectively. From 1984 to 1988, he was an assistant professor at Florida Atlantic University, Boca Raton, FL, where he did graduate work in computer science. In total, he received seven college degrees. From 1988 to 2000, he was at Temple University, Philadelphia, PA, where he became a full professor. From 2000 to 2002, he was with Lucent/Avaya, Holmdel, NJ as a system engineer and with Boeing Satellite Systems, Los Angeles, CA as a senior scientist. He is presently a Regents professor emeritus of electrical and computer engineering at Prairie View A&M University, Prairie View, TX.

He is the author of over 1,530 professional papers and over 160 books including "Elements of Electromagnetics" (Oxford University Press, 7th ed., 2018), "Fundamentals of Electric Circuits" (McGraw-Hill, 7th ed., 2020, with C. Alexander), "Computational Electromagnetics with MATLAB" (CRC Press, 4th ed., 2019), "Principles of Modern Communication Systems" (Cambridge University Press, 2017, with S. O. Agbo), and "Emerging Internet-based Technologies" (CRC Press, 2019). In addition to the engineering books, he has written Christian books including "Secrets of Successful Marriages" (with J. O. Sadiku), "How to Discover God's Will for Your Life," and commentaries on all the books of the New

Testament Bible. Some of his books have been translated into ten languages: French, Korean, Chinese (and Chinese Long Form in Taiwan), Italian, Portuguese, Spanish, German, Dutch, Polish, and Russian.

He was the recipient of the 2000 McGraw-Hill/Jacob Millman Award for outstanding contributions in the field of electrical engineering. He was also the recipient of Regents Professor award for 2012-2013 by the Texas A&M University System. He is a registered professional engineer and a life fellow of the Institute of Electrical and Electronics Engineers (IEEE) "for contributions to computational electromagnetics and engineering education." He was the IEEE Region 2 Student Activities Committee Chairman. He was an associate editor for IEEE Transactions on Education. He is also a member of Association for Computing Machinery (ACM). His current research interests are in the areas of computational electromagnetic, computer science/networks, engineering education, and marriage counseling. His works can be found in his autobiography, "My Life and Work" (Trafford Publishing, 2024) or his website: www.matthew-sadiku.com. He can be reached via email at sadiku@ieee.org.

Part A: Technology

CHAPTER 1

COMPUTATIONAL ENGINEERING

"A computation is a process that obeys finitely describable rules."
– Rudy Rucker

1.1 INTRODUCTION

Today computation is considered an equal partner with theory and experiment. Computation provides a means of studying complex natural phenomena that would be too expensive or dangerous to study by direct experimentation. With the advent of large-scale computers, computational methods and analysis have become indispensable for simulating physical events and engineering systems. Computation has become an integral part of every sector of science and engineering, in addition to the economic, social, and cultural aspects of our daily life [1].

Computational engineering (CE) is a newly emerging multidisciplinary field that applies advanced computational techniques to engineering practice. It embraces engineering, science, applied mathematics, numerical analysis, and computer science. It applies techniques from these areas to solve complex scientific and engineering problems [2].

Computational engineers can build several physical prototypes and test their performance early in the design process. A computational engineer needs to have fundamental knowledge of engineering, advanced mathematics, algorithms, high-performance computing, and computer languages. He must use this knowledge to solve physics-based equations, simulate scenarios, and make predictions. FORTRAN is the most widely used programming language among scientific researchers. Although C++ and C are more recently popular, the scientific computing community has been reluctant to adopt C++ as the lingua franca. MATLAB and Python are also widely used [3].

Computational engineering is a newly emerging interdisciplinary field in engineering that applies advanced computational techniques to solving complex engineering problems. Its main purpose is using computer methods and analysis to solve increasingly complex scientific and engineering problems. Computational prediction is vitally important in making decisions that impact every area of our life [4].

This chapter provides an introduction to computational engineering. The chapter begins with a description of computational modeling. It covers some applications of computational engineering, highlights the benefits and challenges, and concludes with comments.

1.2 COMPUTATIONAL MODELING

Computational modeling usually involves two major steps [5]: (i) modeling of a system, and (ii) solving the resulting model equations using computational techniques. The model will normally allow us to express the behavior of the system in terms of ordinary differential equations (ODEs) or partial differential equations (PDEs). Computational modeling includes using numerical techniques to process, analyze, and visualize data.

There are basically three different numerical techniques available for solving engineering problems [6]:

- The finite-difference method (FDM)
- The finite-element method (FEM)
- The Monte Carlo method (MCM)

The FDM involves the simple discretization of ODEs or PDEs. The FEM is a computational technique that divides the solution region into non-overlapping meshes (or elements), typically triangles in two dimensions and tetrahedra in three dimensions. It is more powerful than FDM. It is the most widely used method for numerical computations in all fields of engineering and can be regarded as a standard tool.

The MCM is a nondeterministic numerical approach, unlike FDM and FEM. It is mostly used for solving stochastic problems.

1.3 APPLICATIONS OF COMPUTATIONAL ENGINEERING

Computational engineering finds diverse applications in many areas, including aircraft design, electronic design automation, weather and climate prediction, predictive surgery, image analysis, trajectory calculation of satellites, battlefield simulation and military gaming, chemical pollution transport, nuclear weapons, computational electromagnetics, energy infrastructure, combustion, risk management and derivative pricing, oil and gas exploration, and particle physics.

For example, the automobile industry improves its products by modeling crashes using high-performance simulation. Manufacturers of integrated circuits (ICs) model their products to minimize defects and power consumption [7].

1.4 BENEFITS AND CHALLENGES

Many companies use CE tools to assist their engineers in analyzing, building, and testing new products because those tools help engineers to be more productive in their work. Computations offer a cost-effective, attractive possibility for investigating and optimizing new products. They also help manufacturers reduce design costs, product cycle time, and time-to-market.

Several companies have replaced the traditional process of design–build–test–and-repeat with physics-based CE tools to design, mesh, and analyze new products with great success. These include Goodyear, GM, Ford, 3M, Procter & Gamble, Whirlpool, Boeing, and Pratt & Whitney [8].

Today, people regard computer-based prediction as very important in making critical decisions that impact every aspect of human existence. However, some companies do not have the expertise to develop their own CE tools; they depend on commercially available packages such as MATLAB, MAPLE, MATHEMATICA, and COMSOL.

Today, meshes with 5 to 100 million elements are becoming feasible. The memory and processing requirements of such a huge mesh size mean that producing interactive displays using a single graphics workstation is difficult, if not impossible.

1.5 CONCLUSION

Computational engineering is a relatively new branch of engineering that embraces engineering, applied mathematics, and computer science. Being a frontier field, practitioners come from different walks of life [9].

The future holds many exciting possibilities for computational engineers. There is a growing need for qualified computational engineers who can efficiently use CE tools to solve complex problems. To meet this need, universities across the world have started offering degrees at undergraduate and graduate levels in CE [10].

More information about CE can be found in [11,12] and in journals exclusively devoted to it:

- *International Journal for Numerical Methods in Engineering*
- *Journal of Computational Methods in Sciences and Engineering*
- *IEEE Computational Science and Engineering*
- *Journal of Computational Engineering*

REFERENCES

[1] Z. Mao and C. Yang, "Computational chemical engineering – Towards thorough understanding and precise application," Chinese Journal of Chemical Engineering, vol. 24, 2016, pp. 945–951.

[2] SIAM Working Group on CSE Education, "Graduate education in computational science and engineering," SIAM Review, vol. 43, no. 1, 2001, pp. 163–177.

[3] "Computational engineering," Wikipedia, the free encyclopedia.

https://en.wikipedia.org/wiki/Computational_engineering

[4] M. N. O. Sadiku, U. C. Chukwu, A. Ajayi-Majebi, and S. M. Musa, "Computational Engineering," IAR Journal of Engineering and Technology, vol. 1, no. 3, 2020, pp. 79–81.

[5] H. Fangohr, Introduction to Python for Computational Science and Engineering (A Beginner's Guide), September 2015. https://www.southampton.ac.uk/~fangohr/training/python/pdfs/Python-for-Computational-Science-and-Engineering.pdf

[6] M. N. O. Sadiku, Computational Electromagnetics with MATLAB, 4th ed., Boca Raton, FL: CRC Press, 2018.

[7] D. E. Post and O. Goldfarb, "Enhancing product innovation with computational engineering," Computing in Science & Engineering, Nov./Dec. 2017, pp. 4–5.

[8] D. Post, "The promise of science-based computational engineering," Computing in Science & Engineering, May/June 2009, pp. 3–4.

[9] C. A. Felippa, "Trends in computational engineering," Advances in Engineering Software, vol. 3, no. 2, 1981, pp. 50–54.

[10] X. Peng et al., "Infusing computational engineering tools in engineering design sequence curricula," Computer-Aided Design and Applications, vol. 7, no. 2, 2010, pp. 183–194.

[11] M. Schäfer, Computational Engineering: Introduction to Numerical Methods. New York, NY: Springer-Verlag, 2006.

[12] G. Hofstetter (ed.), Computational Engineering. Springer-Verlag, 2014.

CHAPTER 2

COMPUTATIONAL MECHANICS

"Computations are everywhere, once you begin to look at things in a certain way."

– Rudy Rucker

2.1 INTRODUCTION

Nowadays, various computational methods are used in all areas of science and engineering. They have been introduced for solving problems in mechanics, heat transfer, electromagnetics, and other areas of physics.

Computational mechanics (CM) refers to the application of numerical methods and digital computers to study phenomena governed by the laws of mechanics. The term computational mechanics has been widely used since 1986, after the 1st World Congress of Computational Mechanics. CM is basically an integral part of computational science and engineering. It is widely regarded as a sub-discipline of applied mechanics or computational science. It has had a profound impact on science and technology over the years. It has transformed much of classical Newtonian theory into practical tools for predicting and understanding complex systems [1].

Computational mechanics (CM) is concerned with the use of computational techniques to characterize, predict, and simulate physical phenomena and engineering systems governed by the principles of mechanics. Over the years, CM has made significant contributions in the design and development of new products and systems [2].

This chapter provides an introduction to computational mechanics. It begins by describing the basic components of computational mechanics. It presents some applications, highlights challenges, and concludes with comments.

2.2 BASIC COMPONENTS

Computational mechanics is an interdisciplinary research field with three major components [3]:

1. **Mechanics:** This includes computational fluid dynamics, computational thermodynamics, computational electromagnetics, computational solid mechanics, solid and structural mechanics, and fluid mechanics.

2. **Mathematics:** CM usually involves developing mathematical models of physical phenomena using partial differential equations, functional analysis, linear algebra, and numerical methods. The most common numerical methods used in CM are the finite element, finite difference, and boundary element methods, in order of their popularity. The finite element method (FEM) is robust, effective, and flexible; it has been thoroughly developed into some commercial and non-commercial software packages such as COMSOL and ABAQUS to handle linear and non-linear mechanics problems.

3. **Computer Science:** Computer programming, algorithms, and parallel computing play a major role in CM. The most widely

used programming languages are FORTRAN and C++. MATLAB and Mathematica are also widely used in the scientific community. Object-oriented programming is becoming common in CM. It proposes that large, complex problems can be broken down into simple, easy-to-manage problems with relatively few concepts: objects, classes, encapsulation, inheritance, and messages. It has been used to capture some abstractions that would have been very hard to express using procedural languages such as FORTRAN or C [4,5].

2.3 APPLICATIONS OF COMPUTATIONAL MECHANICS

CM tools have successfully been used to simulate complex problems that would be difficult, if not impossible, to handle using analytical methods. Examples of practical applications include [1,6]:

- **Vehicle Crash Worthiness:** This involves computer-generated simulation of the crash worthiness of automobiles. It has replaced hundreds of full-scale tests and saved automobile manufacturers several millions of dollars.
- **Predictive Surgery:** CM models are generated for analysis by surgical teams to assist in determining the best procedure for the patient under treatment. The results predicted by these models are used before the actual surgery takes place.
- **Manufacturing:** Modern manufacturing systems are known to be complex. CM provides an opportunity to apply insights to manage complexity in these systems [7].

- **Military Applications:** CM models are used in the analysis and design of weapons and armor.

Other applications include petroleum reservoir modeling, biomechanics, glass manufacturing, semiconductor modeling, environmental modeling, computational wave propagation, bioinformatics and bioengineering, stretchable/compressible electronics, and information fusion.

2.4 CHALLENGES

While it is generally acknowledged that parallel supercomputing offers considerable promise for solving large problems of practical interest, it is essential that some challenges faced by CM are addressed so that it remains competitive.

The reliability of computer-generated predictions is a major concern to CM specialists. The size of the simultaneous linear equations to be solved in CM has been growing larger and larger. Another major challenge in computational mechanics research is bridging the different scales without sacrificing resolution. Modeling events in which the remarkably varying scales are significant in a single system is important.

Computational mechanics also suffers from a lack of modifiability and interactivity. This undermines its potential to help engineers solve problems faster and cheaper. This problem can be tackled by full integration of computer design in CM [8].

CM also faces a general deficiency common to modeling, namely the introduction of errors. In principle, there are two major sources of error in computer simulations of physical phenomena: approximation error, due to the inherent inaccuracies incurred in the discretization of mathematical models; and modeling error, due to the natural imperfections in models of physical phenomena [9,10].

2.5 CONCLUSION

The success of computational mechanics will be determined by its effectiveness in solving real-world problems of interest to society. Future research in CM will be broader than ever before. By incorporating new models of physical and biological systems, CM has great potential for future growth and applicability. It will have a profound impact on many facets of our life, including advances in biology, medicine, energy conservation, and national security.

There are two main organizations committed to promoting CM. The **International Association for Computational Mechanics (IACM)**, based in Spain, provides a common forum for discussion, education, and research information on CM. The **United States Association for Computational Mechanics**, an affiliate of IACM, promotes CM activities in the United States.

More information about CM can be found in the following journals:

- *Computational Mechanics*
- *European Journal of Computational Mechanics*
- *Journal of Applied and Computational Mechanics*
- *Journal of Computational Applied Mechanics*
- *Applied and Computational Mechanics*
- *International Journal for Computational Methods in Engineering.*

REFERENCES

[1] J. T. Oden et al., "Research directions in computational mechanics," *Computer Methods in Applied Mechanics and Engineering*, vol. 192, no. 7–8, Feb. 2003, pp. 913–922.

[2] M. N. O. Sadiku, A. A. Omotoso, and S. M. Musa, "Computational mechanics," *International Journal of Trend in Scientific Research and Development*, vol. 3, no. 2, Jan.–Feb. 2019, pp. 559–560.

[3] "Computational mechanics," *Wikipedia, the free encyclopedia* https://en.wikipedia.org/wiki/Computational_mechanics

[4] J. Whitesell and J. D. Reid, "Computational mechanics solvers based on object-oriented design principles," *Proceedings of the 1990 Winter Simulation Conference*, 1990, pp. 486–489.

[5] R. Sahu, M. J. Panthaki, and W. H. Gerstle, "An object-oriented framework for multidisciplinary, multi-physics, computational mechanics," *Engineering with Computers*, vol. 15, 1999, pp. 105–125.

[6] "What is computational mechanics," *United States Association for Computational Mechanics.*

http://www.usacm.org/what-is-computational-mechanics

[7] R. Vrabic and P. Butala, "Computational mechanics approach to managing complexity in manufacturing systems," *CIRP Annals – Manufacturing Technology*, vol. 60, 2011, pp. 503–506.

[8] S. P. Serna and A. Stork, "Computer design in computational mechanics," *Proceedings of International Conference on Computing, Engineering and Information*, 2009, pp. 329–332.

[9] S. Weihe and B. Kroplin, "Computational mechanics: capabilities and restrictions," *Computational Materials Science*, vol. 16, 1999, pp. 10–16.

[10] J. T. Oden and S. Prudhomme, "Estimation of modeling error in computational mechanics," *Journal of Computational Physics*, vol. 182, 2002, pp. 496–515.

CHAPTER 3

COMPUTATIONAL ELECTROMAGNETICS

"Science never solves a problem without creating ten more."

– George B. Shaw

3.1 INTRODUCTION

Modern society heavily depends on electromagnetic (EM) systems such as radio, television, radar, microwave ovens, mobile telephones, satellite communication systems, the Internet, motors, generators, computers, transformers, and power networks [1]. EM technologies have also benefited other sciences, technology, medicine, the arts, humanities, and many aspects of human civilization.

In the beginning, experts in electromagnetics solved problems with pencil and paper, using largely closed-form analytical solutions. However, in the last 50 years, the EM community has witnessed a breathtaking evolution in the way we solve and apply EM concepts. With the ever-increasing power and memory of digital computers, the art of computational electromagnetics has gained momentum.

Computational electromagnetics (CEM) deals with computational methods applied in solving EM problems. It is based on the computer implementation of mathematical models of EM systems. CEM tools are useful in analyzing and designing power systems, electrical machines, generators, transformers, microwave networks, and antennas. They are also used in predicting electromagnetic compatibility (EMC) between complex electronic systems. For this reason, CEM is of increasing importance to both civil and defense sectors [2].

CEM involves using numerical methods to solve real-life electromagnetic problems. Over the years, a great number of CEM tools have been developed to simulate and analyze electromagnetic systems. This has been made possible due to numerous contributions from institutions, universities, and industries around the world [3].

This chapter provides an introduction to computational electromagnetics. It begins by presenting computational methods, covers computational tools or popular software used in CEM, highlights challenges, and concludes with comments.

3.2 COMPUTATIONAL METHODS

Computational electromagnetics basically involves solving Maxwell's equations [4]:

$$\nabla \bullet \boldsymbol{D} = \rho \tag{1}$$

$$\nabla \bullet \boldsymbol{B} = 0 \tag{2}$$

$$\nabla \times \boldsymbol{E} = -\frac{\partial \boldsymbol{B}}{\partial t} \tag{3}$$

$$\nabla \times \boldsymbol{H} = \boldsymbol{J} + \frac{\partial \boldsymbol{D}}{\partial t} \tag{4}$$

Where **D** and **B** are electric and magnetic flux densities, respectively; **E** and **H** are electric and magnetic field intensities, respectively; and J is the electric current density. These quantities are related as follows:

$$J = \sigma E, \qquad D = \varepsilon E, \qquad B = \mu H \qquad (5)$$

Where σ, ε, and μ are electrical conductivity, permittivity, and permeability of the media.

Maxwell's equations in (1) to (4) define EM wave theory and establish the mathematics of electromagnetic wave–matter interaction. We now discuss the various techniques for solving them.

There are seven common numerical techniques used in electromagnetics [5]:

- **Finite Difference Method:** This involves the discretization of Maxwell's equations in differential form. The finite-difference time-domain (FDTD) method is one of the most widespread in CEM. Although FDTD is efficient, it has difficulties with complex geometries. Applications include scattering, antennas, EMC, and photonics [6].
- **Variational Method:** This involves minimizing a functional defining a given problem. Variational methods are of two types: direct (Rayleigh–Ritz) and indirect (weighted residuals such as collocation, subdomain, Galerkin, and least squares) [7].
- **Moment Method:** This transforms the integral equation of a given problem, by weighted residual techniques, into a matrix equation to be solved numerically. It is suitable for problems involving open regions (scattering, radiation) but has also been

applied successfully to closed problems such as waveguides and cavities [8].

- **Finite Element Method:** This divides the solution region into non-overlapping meshes (triangles in 2D, tetrahedra in 3D). It is more powerful than finite difference methods in handling complex, inhomogeneous media. Its systematic generality makes it possible to develop general-purpose programs for solving a wide variety of problems [9,10].
- **Transmission Line Matrix (TLM) Modeling:** This is a network model of Maxwell's equations formulated in terms of scattering impulses. It discretizes space and time based on the analogy between field propagation and transmission lines. A continuous system is replaced by an array of lumped elements [11,12].
- **Monte Carlo Method:** A nondeterministic numerical approach applied in two ways: simulation (mathematical imitation of random phenomena) and sampling (deducing properties of a set by studying a small random subset). In EM, it is applied as simulation using pseudo-random numbers [13].
- **Method of Lines:** This discretizes a given differential equation in one or two dimensions while using analytical solutions in the remaining direction. It is regarded as a special finite difference method since it combines numerical and analytical techniques. It is computationally efficient, numerically stable, and involves less time since only small discretization is needed [14].

In addition to these, hybrid methods combine low-frequency methods such as those above with high-frequency methods such as the geometric theory of diffraction [15].

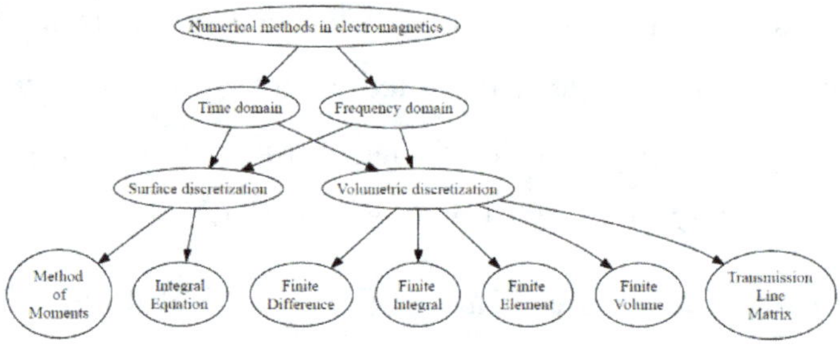

Figure 3.1 - Classification of computational methods [2].

3.3 COMPUTATIONAL TOOLS

Numerical modeling and simulation have revolutionized engineering design to the extent that numerous software packages have been developed. In the 1970s, researchers often had to develop their own programs since very few commercial solvers existed. Today, the situation is completely different. There are dozens of computational tools on the market, and there is no longer strong motivation or need to develop in-house codes in academia or industry.

These commercial packages are attractive due to their graphical interfaces and ability to model real structures in detail. While some are commercial, others are free. Widely used software packages include:

- **COMSOL:** Based on the finite element method; a powerful tool for physics and engineering applications.
- **Numerical Electromagnetic Codes (NEC):** Based on the method of moments; developed at Livermore National Laboratory. It has a PC version (MININEC) and is widely used

for frequency-domain antenna modeling. NEC2 uses a text interface; a free version is *4nec2*.

- **High Frequency Structure Simulator (HFSS):** Based on FEM; developed by Ansoft (later acquired by Ansys). Offers state-of-the-art solvers for a wide range of EM applications.
- **Sonnet:** Provides high-frequency 3D planar EM analysis for single- and multi-layer planar circuits. A free student version (Sonnet Lite) is available.
- **FEKO:** Antenna simulation software based on the method of moments. Calculates radiation pattern, impedance, and gain.
- **EMAP:** A family of 3D electromagnetic modeling codes developed at Missouri University of Science and Technology. Includes EMAP3 (vector FEM) and EMAP5 (vector FEM/MoM).
- **MEEP:** Free, open-source FDTD simulation software developed at MIT (MIT Electromagnetic Equation Propagation). First released in 2006.
- **MaxFem:** An open software package for electromagnetic simulation based on FEM, capable of solving problems in electrostatics, magnetostatics, and eddy currents.

Several more CEM software packages are available, but these are the most popular. These tools place powerful techniques, once limited to specialists, into the hands of engineers not formally trained in CEM. The best choice depends on the problem being solved. Substantial progress has been made in CEM, and further gains continue through these powerful commercial packages.

3.4 CHALLENGES

All CEM techniques have strengths and limitations. Since computation involves discretization, errors are inevitable. Computational accuracy is controlled by the algorithm and the computing resources used. Errors include round-off and truncation. Efficiency can be improved using scalable multicomputers [16].

A well-defined, mature, and robust methodology for validating CEM techniques is essential. Validation is critical: "garbage in, garbage out" (GIGO). Computed results should never be trusted unless verified, at least in part, through measured data, analytical solutions, or results from other methods [17,18].

For CEM methods to solve large-scale electromagnetic boundary-value problems (such as a full-size aircraft at X-band), involving millions of unknowns, a supercomputer or distributed-memory parallel computer is required. A distributed-memory parallel computer consists of independent computers connected through a high-speed network [19]. Multi-scale EM problems, involving both electrically large and small features, can be addressed with software metamaterials [20].

3.5 CONCLUSION

Computational electromagnetics is an interdisciplinary field that combines electromagnetics and scientific computing. Its main objective is to gain insight and understanding based on computer-implemented mathematical models of Maxwell's equations. The field is young, constantly evolving, and has become a major design approach in both industrial and academic research.

The state of the art in CEM is advancing rapidly, supported by specialized journals such as:

- *IEEE Transactions on Microwave Theory and Techniques*
- *Progress in Electromagnetic Research (PIER)*
- *Journal of Electromagnetic Waves and Applications (JEMWA)*
- *Applied Computational Electromagnetics Society Journal*
- *Journal of Computational Physics*

REFERENCES

[1] A. T. Bondeson, T. Rylander, and P. Ingelstrom, Computational Electromagnetics. New York: Springer, 2005, p. 1.

[2] M. Lin and D. W. Walker, "GECEM: A portal-based grid application for computational electromagnetics," Future Generation Computer Systems, vol. 24, Feb. 2008, pp. 66–72.

[3] M. N. O. Sadiku, A. E. Shadare, and S. M. Musa, "Computational electromagnetics," International Journal of Engineering Research, vol. 6, no. 8, Aug. 2017, pp. 414–416.

[4] M. N. O. Sadiku, Elements of Electromagnetics. 6th ed. New York: Oxford University Press, 2015, pp. 407–427.

[5] M. N. O. Sadiku, Numerical Techniques in Electromagnetics with MATLAB. 3rd ed. Boca Raton, FL: CRC Press, 2009.

[6] A. Taflove and S. C. Hagness, Computational Electrodynamics: The Finite-Difference Time-Domain Method. 3rd ed. Boston, MA: Artech House, 2005.

[7] L. Cairo and T. Kahan, Variational Techniques in Electromagnetics. New York: Gordon & Breach, 1965.

[8] R. F. Harrington, Field Computation by Moment Methods. Hoboken, NJ: Wiley-IEEE Press, 1993.

[9] P. P. Silvester and R. L. Ferrari, Finite Elements for Electrical Engineers. 3rd ed. Cambridge, UK: Cambridge University Press, 1996.

[10] J. M. Jin, The Finite Element Method in Electromagnetics. 3rd ed. New York, NY: Wiley, 2014.

[11] C. Christopoulos, The Transmission-Line Modeling Method (TLM). New York: IEEE Press, 1995.

[12] P. Saguet, Numerical Analysis in Electromagnetics: The TLM Method. Hoboken, NJ: Wiley-ISTE Press, 2012.

[13] M. N. O. Sadiku, Monte Carlo Methods for Electromagnetics. Boca Raton, FL: CRC Press, 2009.

[14] R. Pregla, Analysis of Electromagnetic Fields and Waves: The Method of Lines. West Sussex, UK: Wiley, 2008.

[15] L. N. Medgyesi-Mitschang and D. S. Wang, "Hybrid methods in computational electromagnetics: A review," Computer Physics Communications, vol. 68, 1991, pp. 76–94.

[16] J. S. Shang, "Computational Electromagnetics," ACM Computing Surveys, vol. 28, no. 1, Mar. 1996, pp. 97–99.

[17] S. Lange, M. Schaarschmidt, and F. Sabath, "An approach on quality assurance in computational electromagnetic," Proc. of the 2014 International Symposium on Electromagnetic Compatibility (EMC Europe 2014), Gothenburg, Sweden, Sept. 2014, pp. 240–245.

[18] IEEE Electromagnetic Compatibility Society, IEEE Recommended Practice for Validation of Computational Electromagnetics Computer Modeling and Simulations. New York: IEEE, Feb. 2011.

[19] S. Velamparambil, W. C. Chew, and J. Song, "10 Million Unknowns: Is It That Big?" IEEE Antennas and Propagation Magazine, vol. 45, no. 2, Apr. 2003, pp. 43–58.

[20] O. Ozgun and M. Kuzuoglu, "Software metamaterials: Transformation media-based multiscale techniques for computational electromagnetic," Journal of Computational Physics, vol. 236, 2013, pp. 203–219.

CHAPTER 4

COMPUTATIONAL FLUID DYNAMICS

"Computers are good at following instructions, but not at reading your mind."

— Donald Knuth

4.1 INTRODUCTION

Fluid dynamics involves fluid motion and is usually studied in three ways: theoretical analysis, experiment, and numerical analysis (computational fluid dynamics). These three approaches are illustrated in Figure 4.1 [1].

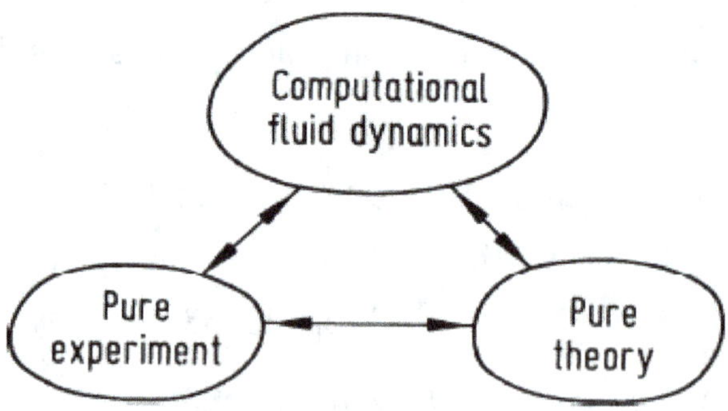

Figure 4.1 - Relationship between CFD, theory, and experiment [1].

Computational fluid dynamics (CFD) is an emerging branch of fluid (gas and liquid) mechanics that applies numerical techniques to solve problems involving fluid flows. It involves the numerical solutions of equations governing the transport of mass, momentum, and energy in moving fluids. In a CFD analysis, fluid flow is examined according to its physical properties such as velocity, pressure, temperature, density, and viscosity.

The basic mathematical description for all CFD problems is given by the Navier–Stokes equations, which represent the conservation of mass, momentum, and energy. These equations describe how the velocity, pressure, temperature, and density of a moving fluid are related. Atmospheric currents, ocean waves, the flow of air around moving vehicles, and the flow of blood through the body are all, in principle, governed by the same set of partial differential equations [2]. At the algorithm level, CFD is similar to computational electromagnetics, computational physics, computational biology, computational chemistry, and many other computational schemes in science and engineering [3].

CFD is essentially based on the Navier–Stokes equations, which describe the motion of viscous fluids. It involves solving a set of transport equations using numerical techniques such as the finite difference method and the finite element method. It is now a key design tool for mechanical engineers [4].

This chapter presents an introduction to CFD. It begins with the basic procedure, provides some applications, highlights challenges, and concludes with comments.

4.2 BASIC PROCEDURE

Commercial software packages for solving CFD problems include COMSOL, ANSYS, CFX, and STAR-CCM. These codes are capable of producing accurate solutions of flows. All CFD codes have three elements: (1) a preprocessor, (2) a flow solver, and (3) a post-processor. The application of CFD to analyze a fluid problem generally requires the following steps [5]:

- **Preprocessing:** The problem geometry is input. The physical geometry and boundary or initial conditions are specified using computer-aided design (CAD). The volume occupied by the fluid is divided into discrete cells (mesh). The mesh may be uniform or non-uniform, structured or unstructured, consisting of combinations of hexahedral, tetrahedral, prismatic, pyramidal, or polyhedral elements. The equations of fluid motion and the material parameters are also defined.
- **Processing (Simulation):** The partial differential equations describing the problem are solved iteratively as steady-state or transient. Different methods may be used by the solver, including the finite volume method (FVM), finite element method (FEM), finite difference method (FDM), spectral element method, and boundary element method.
- **Postprocessing:** Simulation results are processed to extract the desired information, such as forces and other quantities of interest. This is used for analysis and visualization of results.

4.3 APPLICATIONS

CFD is widely applied in areas of fluid and heat transfer. It is used in automotive, aerospace, biomedical, marine, oil and gas, hydraulics, chemical processing, the food industry, and any field where fluid motion plays a critical role. Applications of CFD include [6,7]:

- Flow and heat transfer in industrial processes (boilers, combustion equipment, heat exchangers, etc.)
- Aerodynamics of ground vehicles, aircraft, and missiles
- Heating, cooling, and ventilation flows in buildings
- Modeling blood flow in the heart and vessels and in heart-assist devices
- Simulation of blood flow in the human heart
- Simulation of gas flow in models of the human lung
- Simulation of many processes in the food industry
- Simulation for spray-freezing in a cold gas
- Simulation of different parts of industrial freeze-drying equipment
- Design and characterization of cooling systems in electrical machines
- Circuit-breaker flow analysis
- Fire and smoke modeling in buildings
- Simulation and analysis of greenhouse solar dryers

4.4 BENEFITS AND CHALLENGES

CFD has relatively low cost compared to physical experiments, is fast, can simulate real conditions, handle complex problems, and yield a comprehensive set of parameters for examination. Although some tools for solving CFD problems are commercially available, their strengths must always be weighed against their limitations when making decisions. The danger lies in using the tools as a black box, inputting data to produce output without awareness of limitations.

One must be careful when interpreting results produced by CFD techniques because many potential sources of error may be involved. Solving problems using computers introduces numerical errors such as truncation and round-off errors.

4.5 CONCLUSION

Computational fluid dynamics uses numerical tools to simulate and analyze problems involving fluid flow. It has evolved from being a research tool to a powerful design tool. It is regarded as the new "third dimension" in fluid dynamics, the other two dimensions being theory and experiment. Since many interesting fluid problems require large amounts of time, parallel CFD models have been developed to significantly reduce computation time [8].

CFD has gained acceptance in engineering education at both graduate and undergraduate levels. Students often use FORTRAN, MATLAB, or Excel spreadsheets to solve problems and are exposed to commercial CFD packages [9,10]. For more information on CFD, one should consult [1,11–17].

REFERENCES

[1] J. F. Wendt (ed.), Computational Fluid Dynamics: An Introduction. 3rd ed. Berlin: Springer, 2009, p. 7.

[2] A. Quarteroni et al., "Computational fluid dynamics at CRS4, Italy," Computing in Science & Engineering, May/June 2012, pp. 10–19.

[3] A. Khajeh-Saeed and J. B. Perot, "Computational fluid dynamics simulation using many graphics processors," Computing in Science & Engineering, May/June 2012, pp. 10–19.

[4] M. N. O. Sadiku, Y. Wang, S. Cui, and S. M. Musa, "Computational fluid dynamics," International Journal of Advanced Engineering and Technology, vol. 2, no. 2, May 2018, pp. 40–41.

[5] "Computational fluid dynamics," Wikipedia, the free encyclopedia
https://en.wikipedia.org/wiki/Computational_fluid_dynamics

[6] A. Bakker, "Applied computation fluid dynamics," http://www.bakker.org

[7] C. L. Lin et al., "Computational fluid dynamics," IEEE Engineering in Medicine and Biology Magazine, May/June 2009, pp. 25–33.

[8] S. Succi and F. Papetti, An Introduction to Parallel Computational Fluid Dynamics. Commack, NY: Nova Science Publishers, 1997.

[9] D. Adair and M. Jaeger, "Incorporating computational fluid dynamics code development into an undergraduate engineering

course," International Journal of Mechanical Engineering Education, vol. 43, no. 3, 2015, pp. 153–167.

[10] T. Barber and V. Timchenko, "Student-specific projects for greater engagement in a computational fluid dynamics course," Australasian Journal of Engineering Education, vol. 17, no. 2, 2011, pp. 129–138.

[11] R. Lohner, Applied Computational Fluid Dynamics Techniques: An Introduction Based on Finite Element Methods. Chichester, UK: John Wiley & Sons, 2008.

[12] A. Sharma, Introduction to Computational Fluid Dynamics: Development, Application and Analysis. John Wiley & Sons, 2017.

[13] J. Tu, G. H. Yeoh, and C. Liu, Computational Fluid Dynamics. 3rd ed. Elsevier, 2019.

[14] H. K. Versteeg and W. Malalasekera, An Introduction to Computational Fluid Dynamics: The Finite Volume Method. 2nd ed. Essex, UK: Prentice Education, 2007.

[15] B. Andersson et al., Computational Fluid Dynamics for Engineers. New York: Cambridge University Press, 2012.

[16] P. J. Roache, Fundamentals of Computational Fluid Dynamics. Hermosa Publishers, 1998.

[17] M. B. Abbott and D. R. Basco, Computational Fluid Dynamics – An Introduction for Engineers. John Wiley & Sons, 1989.

CHAPTER 5

COMPUTATIONAL NANOTECHNOLOGY

"Everybody in this country should learn to program a computer, because it teaches you how to think."

– Steve Jobs

5.1 INTRODUCTION

Nanotechnology, the science of tiny things at the nanoscale, may be the new frontier in the transformation of every sector, from medicine to the food industry. The 21st century is regarded as the century of nanotechnology. The applications of nanotechnology have become vast, covering a wide range of fields including materials, electronics, photonics, biotechnology, life sciences, industry, food, agriculture, medicine, energy, transportation, and defense/military, etc. The past two decades have witnessed how nanotechnology has progressed from academics and the laboratory research phase to use in various commercial applications. The research activities on nanotechnology are increasing globally at a rapid rate with almost no nation left behind. Industries and governments across the world are investing heavily in nanotechnology [1].

The development of algorithms and computational tools for the progress of nanoscience and nanotechnology has created an emerging research area known as computational nanotechnology.

Computational nanotechnology (or computational nanoscience) arose in the 1990s as a synthesis of computational chemistry and computational nanotechnology, infused by people and practices from computational materials science, engineering, computer science, etc. Since then, computational nanotechnology has been a part of research. The goal of computational nanotechnology is to develop theory, models, and simulations [2].

In nanotechnology, computer simulations are important due to two main reasons. One is the difficulty in conducting actual experiments at this length scale. The second reason is that, even though in some cases the conventional theoretical models are valid, the inability to solve these models by incorporating all the complexities has brought in new challenges [3].

Nanotechnology has led to significant innovations in the diverse areas of electronics, microcomputing, and biotechnology to medicine, consumer supplies, aerospace, and energy production. Computational nanotechnology is the study, design, and optimization of nanoscale systems. It is a powerful tool for understanding nanoparticle physics and chemistry. It enables tools and techniques for physics- and chemistry-based simulation [4].

This chapter provides a primer on computational nanotechnology. It begins with providing an overview of nanotechnology. It covers computational nanotechnology and the network for computational nanotechnology. It highlights some benefits and challenges of computational nanotechnology. The last section concludes with comments.

5.2 OVERVIEW OF NANOTECHNOLOGY

Nano is a prefix that indicates one billionth of a specified parameter. Nanotechnology is the engineering of systems at the molecular or nanoscale. It has been called the second Industrial Revolution because of the special properties of materials at the nanoscale. It is a branch of green technology which has the potential to revolutionize many aspects of our lives. It has permeated all sectors of our economy due to the unique properties of materials at the nanoscale. It is transforming the world of materials and its influence will be broad. It will not only initiate the next industrial revolution, it will offer technological solutions. Nanocomputing is part of the emerging field of nanotechnology.

Richard Feynman, a famous Nobel Laureate physicist, is regarded as the father of nanotechnology. Nanotechnology has provided effective processing features, miniaturization from micro to nano obeying Moore's law, which states that CPU performance is doubled every 18 months [5]. Nanotechnology is the science of small things, at the atomic level or nanoscale level. It has the idea that the technology of the future will be built on atoms. It has an impact on every area of science and technology [6].

Nanotechnology involves imaging, measuring, modeling, and manipulating matter at the nanoscale. It covers a wide variety of disciplines like physics, chemistry, biology, biotechnology, information technology, engineering, and their potential applications.

Nanotechnology has a vast range of applications, such as in nanomedicine, nanoelectronics, biomaterials, energy production, and consumer products. It is revolutionizing many industry sectors: information technology, homeland security, medicine, transportation, energy, food safety, and environmental science. In medicine, for example, nanotechnology is broadening the medical tools, knowledge, and therapies currently available to medical professionals. It can lead to creating smart drugs. Gold nanoparticles are being investigated as potential treatments for cancer and other diseases.

Nanoparticles are used increasingly in catalysis to boost chemical reactions, especially in petroleum refining and automotive catalytic converters. Nanotechnology will likely revolutionize sensor capabilities. Nanosensors and nanoactuators have the potential for improving the capability of sensor networks. Applications of nanotechnology are illustrated in Figure 5.1.

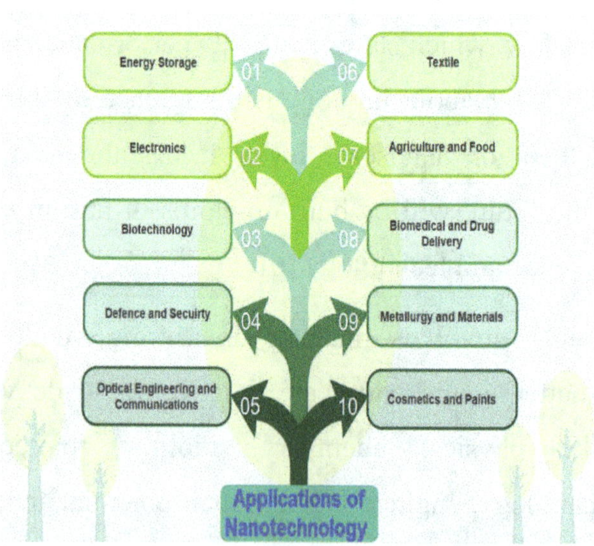

Figure 5.1 - Applications of nanotechnology.

5.3 COMPUTATIONAL NANOTECHNOLOGY

Nanotechnology is applied in many scientific and practical applications, including medicine, agriculture, electronic devices, computer science, and many other fields. Figure 5.2 shows the subfields of computational nanotechnology [7].

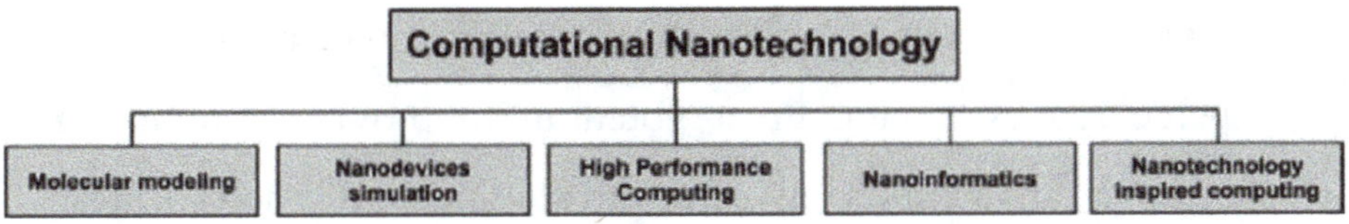

Figure 5.2 - Subfields of computational nanotechnology [7].

Computational nanotechnology is used in predicting the toxicity caused due to different nanomaterials. It plays a major role in developing next generation multifunctional materials, molecular-scale electronic and computing devices, sensors, actuators, and machines. Other applications of computational models in nanotechnology include the following [8]:

- **Medicine:** Computational models are used in various areas of medicine such as management of psychic disorders, cardiovascular diseases, brain diseases, cancer, diabetes, personalized medicine, etc. Computational modeling of physiological processes is crucial to comprehending complicated physiological phenomena accurately. Multiple computational techniques are utilized in the medical field to create, improve, or to accelerate new drug development, creating the foundation of computer-aided medicine discovery. Computational modeling techniques also help us understand the causes of disease at a profound level. Recently, the US Food and Drug Administration (FDA) used computational techniques to design different medical devices, which might aid in identifying and correcting issues during the formulation stage before the formulation is released into the market.

- **Drug Delivery:** Nanoscience and nanotechnology are perceived as having great potential to provide benefits in several areas such as the development of new drugs. Mathematical models have been used to explain experimental findings in drug delivery and to extrapolate these experimental findings to larger populations. Computational models are applied in the development of nanoparticle and other organic and inorganic nanocarriers useful in drug delivery. Computational modeling has also shown its importance in pharmacokinetic studies.
- **Imaging:** Experimental methods and medical imaging advancements have shown the importance and application of computational modeling in imaging study.
- **Nano-Engineered Electronic Device:** This involves developing computation and simulation tools that can be employed for turning nanoscale science and engineering into applications through the discovery and development of nanoelectronic-based devices.
- **Computational Nanoelectronics:** It develops and applies numerical algorithms to investigate nanodevices ranging from

next-generation transistors to thermoelectric generators and optoelectronic devices. While theories based on classical physics have been very successful in helping experimentalists design microelectronic devices, new approaches based on quantum mechanics are required to accurately model today's nanoscale transistors and solar cells and to predict their characteristics even before they are fabricated.

- **Computational Nanomechanics:** The role of computational nanomechanics has become critically important in the cycle of growth and development of nanotechnology, because the length and time scales of important nanoscale systems and phenomena have shrunk to the level where they can be directly addressed with high-fidelity computer simulations.

5.4 NETWORK FOR COMPUTATIONAL NANOTECHNOLOGY

The Network for **Computational Nanotechnology (NCN)** is a multi-university center sponsored by the National Science Foundation to develop models and simulation tools to predict behavior at the device, circuit, and system level for nanoelectronics, nanoelectromechanics, and nanobio systems. Founded in 2002, the Network for Computational Nanotechnology (NCN) has pursued its mission to advance nanoscience and nanotechnology. The Purdue University-led cyber platform, nanoHUB, assists researchers across the globe by developing a virtual society. nanoHUB.org is recognized as the world's largest nanotechnology user facility. It facilitates fast knowledge transfer across countries, disciplines, and communities.

Annually, nearly 250,000 users in 172 countries participate in nanoHUB, an online meeting place for simulation, research, collaboration, teaching, learning, and publishing [9,10]. **nanoHUB** is shown in Figure 5.3 [11].

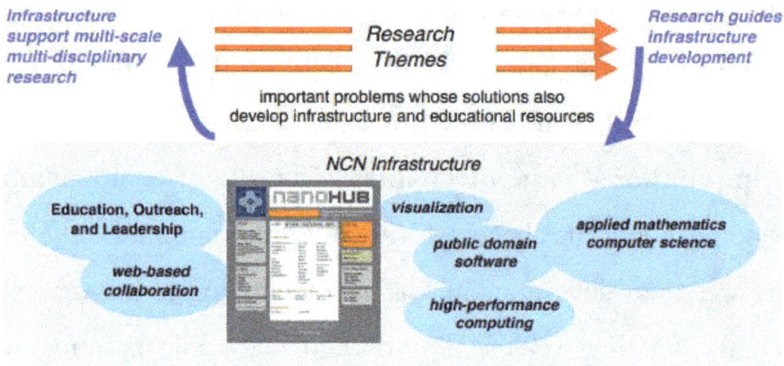

Figure 5.3 - nanoHub [11].

The goals of NCN are to [12]: (1) accelerate the transformation of nanoscience to nanotechnology through the integration of simulation with experimentation; (2) engage an ever-larger and more diverse cyber community sharing novel, high-quality nanoscale computation and simulation research and educational resources; (3) develop open-access, open-source software to stimulate data sharing; and (4) inspire and educate the next-generation workforce. The NCN consists of a stand-alone cyber platform, which provides computation, simulation, and education services to over 330,000 researchers, educators, students, and industry members of the nanoscience and engineering community annually worldwide.

5.5 BENEFITS

In this era, nanoscience progresses in every aspect of science, and nanotechnologies make life easier. Every research discipline benefits from nanotechnology, including physics, chemistry, biology, material science, computer science, and engineering. Nanotechnology has several advantages, such as superior surface area and nano-sized molecular structure. Nanomaterials have a higher energy storage capacity than coarse-grained compounds. They have the capability to store high energy, which makes them applicable in the healthcare system. Computational modeling of nanocompounds is a powerful tool to identify their fundamental characteristics. As a result of the potential integration of photons, atoms, and biological cells via nanotechnology, new prospects have opened up for companies [8].

5.6 CHALLENGES

Although computational-modeling techniques are increasingly popular, there are challenges to overcome before they may be used in clinical practice. The integration of heterogeneous data from many sources and classes is a challenge. Computational modeling is regarded as less cumulative than other forms of study. It involves multiple simplifications, which may fail to capture all crucial features, creating issues associated with the model's validity. Some contend that computational models do not really advance our understanding because they are too complex to understand why they behave the way they do [8]. Improved technology is required to achieve a more robust quantitative understanding of matter at the nanoscale. Functional nanotechnology, nanoelectronics, nanofabrication, manufacturing, quantum engineering, and producing nanomaterials such as graphene and carbon nanotubes are all key skills that need to be developed.

5.7 CONCLUSION

Nanotechnology is the aptitude to perceive, measure, operate, and build materials at the nanometer scale, the size of atoms and molecules. It deals with materials, devices, and their applications in areas such as engineered materials, electronics, computers, sensors, actuators, and machines, at the nano length-scale. It plays a growing important role in understanding mechanical properties at such a small scale. Nanotechnology has promised a great future for humanity.

Computational nanotechnology is emerging as a fundamental engineering analysis tool for the novel designs of nanodevices. It encompasses not only research into these exciting new computer technologies but also how to build them. This new manufacturing technology will usher in new possibilities in computation: molecular electronics, quantum cellular automata, DNA computing, single-electron switches, adiabatic computing, quantum computing, and more. More information about computational nanotechnology can be found in the books in [1,13–25] and the following related journals:

- *Nanotechnology*
- *Computational Nanotechnology*
- *The IEEE Open Journal of Nanotechnology*
- *Journal of Computational and Theoretical Nanoscience*

REFERENCES

[1] M. N. O. Sadiku, S. M. Musa, T. J. Ashaolu, and J. O. Sadiku, Applications of Nanotechnology. Gotham Books, 2023, p. 5.

[2] M. Safdar, "Computational nanotechnology: Its goal, approach, role and scope."

https://biotecharticles.com/Nanotechnology-Article/COMPUTATIONAL-NANOTECHNOLOGY-Its-Goal-Approach-Role-and-Scope-430.html

[3] "Computational nanotechnology."

https://intranet.cb.amrita.edu/sites/default/files/ME806-Computational_Nanotechnology.pdf

[4] M. N. O. Sadiku, U. C. Chukwu, and J. O. Sadiku, "Computational nanotechnology," World of Science: Journal on Modern Research Methodologies, vol. 2, no. 12, 2023, pp. 98–104.

[5] R. Yadav, C. K. Dixit, and S. K. Trivedi, "Nanotechnology and nano computing," International Journal for Research in Applied Science & Engineering Technology, vol. 5, no. X, Oct. 2017.

[6] M. N. O. Sadiku, M. Tembely, and S. M. Musa, "Nanotechnology: An introduction," International Journal of Software and Hardware Research in Engineering, vol. 4, no. 5, May 2016, pp. 40–44.

[7] O. P. V. Neto, "Intelligent computational nanotechnology: The role of computational intelligence in the development of nanoscience and nanotechnology," Journal of Computational and Theoretical Nanoscience, vol. 11, 2014, pp. 1–17.

[8] A. Rajput et al., “Computational nanoscience and technology,” OpenNano, vol. 12, July 2023.

[9] G. Klimeck et al., “Network for Computational Nanotechnology – A strategic plan for global knowledge transfer in research and education,” 2011 IEEE Nanotechnology Materials and Devices Conference, Oct. 2011.

[10] “Network for Computational Nanotechnology.”

https://trynano.org/organizational-spotlight/network-for-computational-nanotechnology/

[11] “NSF Network for Computational Nanotechnology.” Dec. 2002.

https://www.nseresearch.org/2002/NewFiles/Over53_NCN.pdf

[12] “Network for Computational Nanotechnology.”

https://new.nsf.gov/funding/opportunities/network-computational-nanotechnology/505317

[13] S. M. Musa (ed.), Computational Nanotechnology: Modeling and Applications with MATLAB. Boca Raton, FL: CRC Press, 2018.

[14] S. M. Musa (ed.), Computational Finite Element Methods in Nanotechnology. Boca Raton, FL: CRC Press, 2012.

[15] A. Taflove, A. Oskooi, and S. G. Johnson (eds.), Advances in FDTD Computational Electrodynamics: Photonics and Nanotechnology. Boston, MA: Artech House, 2013.

[16] J. R. Reimers, Computational Methods for Large Systems: Electronic Structure Approaches for Biotechnology and Nanotechnology. Hoboken, NJ: John Wiley & Sons, 2011.

[17] F. A. Buot, Nonequilibrium Quantum Transport Physics in Nanosystems: Foundation of Computational Nonequilibrium Physics in Nanoscience and Nanotechnology. World Scientific, 2009.

[18] V. Barone (ed.), Computational Strategies for Spectroscopy: From Small Molecules to Nano Systems. Hoboken, NJ: John Wiley & Sons, 2011.

[19] M. D. Dadmun et al. (eds.), Computational Studies, Nanotechnology, and Solution Thermodynamics of Polymer Systems. New York: Kluwer Academic/Plenum Publishers, 2001.

[20] M. Rieth and W. Schommers (eds.), Handbook of Theoretical and Computational Nanotechnology. American Scientific Publishers, 2006.

[21] R. R. Letfullin and T. F. George, Computational Nanomedicine and Nanotechnology: Lectures with Computer Practicums. Cham: Springer, 2018.

[22] Technical Proceedings of the 2002 International Conference on Computational Nanoscience and Nanotechnology, Puerto Rico, Apr. 2002.

[23] B. Asthana, Computational Nanotechnology. Westbury Publishing Ltd., 2023.

[24] J. Y. Hsu, Nanocomputing: Computational Physics for Nanoscience and Nanotechnology. Singapore: Jenny Stanford Publishing, 2009.

[25] A. K. Haghi, F. Naghiyev, and S. Abdullayeva (eds.), Advanced Computational Techniques in Nanoscience (Nanotechnology Science and Technology). UK: Nova Science Publishers, 2013.

Part B:
Natural Sciences

CHAPTER 6

COMPUTATIONAL BIOLOGY

"The real danger is not that computers will begin to think like men, but that men will begin to think like computers."

— Sydney J. Harris

6.1 INTRODUCTION

With the advent of digital computers, several fields discovered the potential of employing their capacities in storage, computation, and simulation. The computation era has exploded and generated new research areas that go beyond all expectations. One such area is computational biology [1]. Several aspects of biology cannot be studied without the power of computers. Algorithms of specific interest to biologists, such as BLAST (developed by Stephen Altschul in 1990) and FASTA (developed by William Pearson in 1988), could not be applied without computers. It has been argued that computational thinking and computational methods are so crucial to understanding life that today all biology is regarded as computational biology. Biological knowledge is now defined, organized, and accessed through computation [2].

Computational biology is the science of using biological data to develop models to understand various biological systems. It is not to be confused with biological computation, which is a branch of computer science that employs biology to build computers. It is similar to bioinformatics, an interdisciplinary science that uses computers to process biological data. It may also be regarded as a subfield of evolutionary computation [3]. Computational biology spans several classical areas such as biology, chemistry, physics, mathematics, and computer science.

Computation is an integral part of a larger revolution that is affecting how science is conducted. Computational biology is an important emerging field uniquely enabled by computation. It involves using computers to model biological problems and interpret data, especially in evolutionary and molecular biology. The application of computational tools to biology is producing new insights into problems too complex for conventional approaches [4].

This chapter introduces computational biology. It explains computational concepts, provides some applications, describes the role of a computational biologist, and concludes with comments.

6.2 COMPUTATIONAL CONCEPTS

Efficient algorithms have always been of primary importance in computational biology. An algorithm is primarily developed to solve the problem it is intended for. With modern computers, an algorithm can be turned into a computer program or code, instructing the computer how to solve a given problem. It is essentially a series of steps used in problem solving.

Constructing algorithms in computational biology usually consists of two steps. The first step is to construct a model of the biological reality. The second step is to construct an algorithm that solves the computational problem defined by the model. Thus, computational biologists often face two tasks: mathematical formulation and skillful programming. The specific details of the model and algorithm depend on the questions being addressed [4].

6.3 APPLICATIONS

Computational biology is generally associated with practical applications. It applies mathematical modeling and computational simulation techniques to the study of biological systems. The following application areas illustrate its impact on biology:

- **Nanobiotechnology:** Computational algorithms can be used to solve problems in specialized fields such as molecular nanobiotechnology. Nanoscale is the natural realm of molecules, proteins, DNA, RNA, and other components of the biological cell.
- **Stem Cell Biology:** Computational tools have played incisive roles in developmental stem cell biology. Computational stem cell biology has emerged as a discipline concerned with synthesizing systems-level modeling of stem cells with large-scale molecular data [5].
- **Sequence Comparison:** This is one of the principal techniques used by computational biologists. The most popular tool for this purpose is BLAST (Basic Local Alignment Search Tool), which performs comparisons between pairs of sequences [6].

- **Drug Discovery:** Drug discovery is impossible without sophisticated modeling and computation. Computational methods have been successfully applied throughout the process, from clinical data to building network models of molecular processes [7].

Other applications include RNA and protein structure prediction, genome sequence alignment, regulatory genomics, image analysis, context-free grammar recognition, and optimal static search tree construction.

Most of these applications are data-intensive, require large runtime and memory, and can readily benefit from parallel computing [8]. In fact, computational biology is one of the most exciting research areas in which high-performance computing (HPC) finds application. It encourages the use of many parallelism-based technologies: multicore computing, cluster computing, supercomputing, cloud computing, grid computing, and green computing [9].

6.4 COMPUTATIONAL BIOLOGIST

Computational biology is an interdisciplinary field that includes systems biology, genomics, molecular networks, population genetics, and bioinformatics. It involves biomedical scientists, engineers, and clinicians working together to combine modern computational techniques.

A computational biologist is an expert in at least two fields (biology and computer science) in order to understand a biological problem and then design, test, and implement a computer-aided approach to solve that problem [6]. A computational biologist may be a mathematical modeler, bioinformaticist, software developer, or data analyst. Much of their time is spent analyzing and interpreting data. They must be skilled at selecting and using appropriate software and thoroughly familiar with it. Sound knowledge of biology is essential to properly interpret computational results. It is always expedient to compare results with those from another approach (another computational method or experiment) to gain confidence in the findings.

6.5 CONCLUSION

Computational biology is a branch of biology concerned with utilizing the capacities of computers to address problems of biological interest. It is defined by the techniques that computer science brings to the formulation and solving of challenging problems. The field has expanded rapidly in the last few years.

Academic institutions have started to offer graduate programs in computational biology [10]. Given the broad nature of the field, it is impossible for students to master all its complexities or gain a background in every area. Students specializing in computational biology should obtain broad, interdisciplinary knowledge of fundamental principles in biology, computational science, statistics, and mathematics. They may also need programming skills in C++, Python, and MATLAB. Graduates can look forward to career prospects in all areas of biomedical sciences.

The field of computational biology has a bright future. For more information, one should consult the books in [11–14] and other references available. Three international journals exclusively devoted to the field are:

- *Journal of Computational Biology*
- *PLoS Computational Biology*
- *IEEE/ACM Transactions on Computational Biology and Bioinformatics*

These journals will help readers stay on top of this rapidly developing discipline.

REFERENCES

[1] R. B. Lyngsø, "Computational biology," Doctoral Dissertation, University of Aarhus, Denmark, 2000.

[2] F. Markowetz, "All biology is computational biology," PLOS Biology, vol. 15, no. 3, Mar. 2017.

[3] "Computational biology."

https://en.wikipedia.org/wiki/Computational_biology

[4] C. N. S. Pedersen, "Algorithms in computational biology," Doctoral Dissertation, University of Aarhus, Denmark, 2000.

[5] Q. Bian and P. Cahan, "Computational tools for stem cell biology," Trends in Biotechnology, vol. 34, no. 12, Dec. 2016, pp. 993–1009.

[6] H. R. Garner and A. Pertsemlidis, "Computational biology: Biological insight from 1s and 0s," BIOSILICO, vol. 1, no. 1, Mar. 2003, pp. 27–35.

[7] L. Yao, J. A. Evans, and A. Rzhetsky, "Novel opportunities for computational biology and sociology in drug discovery," Trends in Biotechnology, vol. 27, no. 9, Aug. 2009, pp. 531–540.

[8] S. Aluru, "Computational biology on parallel computers," Proceedings of the European Control Conference, Cambridge, UK, Sept. 2003.

[9] M. A. Vega-Rodríguez and A. Rubio-Largo, "Parallelism in computational biology: A view from diverse high-performance

computing applications," The International Journal of High Performance Computing Applications, 2016, pp. 1–4.

[10] M. Gerstein, "An interdepartmental Ph.D. program in computational biology and bioinformatics: The Yale perspective," Journal of Biomedical Informatics, vol. 40, 2007, pp. 73–79.

[11] B. Haubold and T. Wiehe, Introduction to Computational Biology: An Evolutionary Approach. Springer, 2006.

[12] M. S. Waterman, Introduction to Computational Biology: Maps, Sequences and Genomes. London, UK: Chapman & Hall, 1995.

[13] G. B. Singh, Fundamentals of Bioinformatics and Computational Biology: Methods and Exercises in MATLAB. Springer, 2015.

[14] J. M. Hanrock and M. Zvelebil, Dictionary of Bioinformatics and Computational Biology. Hoboken, NJ: John Wiley & Sons, 2004.

CHAPTER 7

COMPUTATIONAL PHYSICS

"The purpose of computing is insight, not numbers."

— Richard W. Hamming

7.1 INTRODUCTION

Since the beginning of the computer era, physicists have been at the forefront of computational science. They used computers to solve a practical problem important at that moment: the development of thermonuclear weapons. The work was implemented on the MANIAC I mainframe computer in Los Alamos [1].

Computational physics (CP) is part of the general area of computational science. It applies numerical methods to solving physical problems. It supplements theoretical physics and experimental physics, the three common ways of solving problems in physics. Since most physics problems are difficult to solve exactly or are nonlinear in nature, CP involves computer simulation and is often regarded as "computer experiments."

It is possible to find a computational branch for every field in physics, e.g., computational mechanics, computational electromagnetics, computational electrodynamics, computational fluid dynamics, computational statistical physics, computational particle physics, computational astrophysics, and computational solid-state physics [2,3]. Topics covered in a regular course on CP include differentiation, integration, Fourier analysis, data fitting, nonlinear least-squares fitting, Monte Carlo methods, and the Runge–Kutta method [4].

Computers are playing an increasingly important role in the lives and education of physicists. Several areas in physics involve problems that cannot be treated exactly or analytically and must be solved numerically. Computational physics enables the development of models of physical phenomena and fosters deeper understanding than is otherwise possible. It also allows learning physics with computers [5].

This chapter provides an introduction to computational physics. It begins with the roles of computational physics, covers some applications, highlights challenges, and concludes with comments.

7.2 ROLES OF COMPUTATIONAL PHYSICS

Besides its application to studying physical phenomena, computational physics plays other key roles [6]:

- It develops our understanding of basic physics and clarifies the importance of physical effects.
- It enables the development of models of physical phenomena and understanding at deeper levels than otherwise possible.
- It solves actual physical problems, whether small-scale or large.
- It helps us learn to compute better and to ask more penetrating, relevant questions.

7.3 APPLICATIONS

Computational physics provides solutions to linear and nonlinear systems of equations, ordinary and partial differential equations, Fourier transforms, stochastic processes, and Monte Carlo methods.

Depending on whether the researcher is a digital native or a digital immigrant, programming languages used in computational physics include FORTRAN, C, C++, and Python. The researcher develops self-contained programs in any of these high-level scientific languages. One may also use mathematical software packages such as MATHEMATICA, MAPLE, EXCEL, or MATLAB. A thorough discussion of these languages and software packages can be found in [7].

7.4 CHALLENGES

In spite of the several CP textbooks available, developing a curriculum that includes computational physics in a meaningful way is not straightforward. Instructors may be compelled to teach topics that should normally be covered in mathematics and computer science since students may not be adequately prepared in those areas. Figure 7.1 shows the relationship between CP and other disciplines [2].

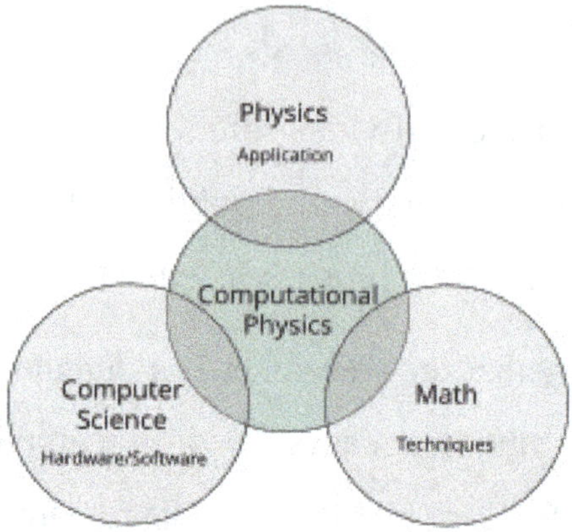

Figure 7.1 - Relationship between CP and other related disciplines [2].

Another problem is deciding whether students should program themselves or use existing software. One may assume that commercially available software packages are the best method for student work because they prevent students from becoming bogged down in direct programming. However, experience shows that some packages may be difficult to use and may distract students from learning [8].

It is recommended that students be allowed to use advanced computational tools only for investigating complex physical phenomena appropriate for building virtual laboratories. Simulation in a virtual laboratory helps in understanding complicated processes [9].

7.5 CONCLUSION

Physicists have realized the power of computation in both research and education. They have integrated CP into physics curricula and written CP textbooks [10]. Some universities even offer a four-year curriculum leading to a bachelor's degree in computational physics

[11]. Although only time will judge the viability of such programs, a carefully developed course on CP can contribute to the goals of a liberal arts curriculum in a unique manner.

Computational knowledge is also transmitted from one researcher to another through conferences and journals. The Journal of Computational Physics publishes research on all aspects of the numerical solution of physical problems.

REFERENCES

[1] L. N. Shchur, "Computational physics and testing theoretical predictions," Uspekhi Fizicheskikh Nauk, vol. 182, no. 7, 2012, pp. 733–738.

[2] "Computational physics."

https://en.wikipedia.org/wiki/Computational_physics

[3] M. N. O. Sadiku, Computational Electromagnetics with MATLAB. 4th ed. Boca Raton, FL: CRC Press, 2018.

[4] R. H. Landau and M. J. Paez, Computational Physics: Problem Solving with Computers. New York: John Wiley & Sons, 1997.

[5] M. N. O. Sadiku, A. E. Shadare, and S. M. Musa, "Computational physics: An introduction," International Journal of Engineering Research, vol. 6, no. 9, Sept. 2017, pp. 427–428.

[6] A. Prosperetti and G. Tryggvason, "Appendix 3: Report of study group on computational physics," International Journal of Multiphase Flow, vol. 29, 2003, pp. 1089–1099.

[7] R. Fitzpatrick, Computational Physics. CreateSpace Independent Publishing Platform, 2015, pp. 7–12.

[8] R. F. Martin, "Undergraduate computational physics education: Uneven history and promising future," Computing in Science & Engineering, Mar./Apr. 2017, pp. 70–78.

[9] K. R. Roos, "An incremental approach to computational physics education," Computing in Science & Engineering, Sept./Oct. 2006, pp. 44–50.

[10] L. Andrasik, "Computational qualitative economics – Using computational intelligence for advanced learning of economics in knowledge society," Creative and Knowledge Society, vol. 5, no. 2, 2015, pp. 1–15.

[11] R. H. Landau, "Computational physics for undergraduates," Computing in Science & Engineering, Mar./Apr. 2004, pp. 68–75.

CHAPTER 8

COMPUTATIONAL CHEMISTRY

"Computations: No one believes them, except the person who makes them. Experiments: Everyone believes them, except the person who made them."

— B. Munk

8.1 INTRODUCTION

Many disciplines have undergone a computational turn in the past decades. The recent computational turn has produced subdisciplines such as computational humanities, computational sociology, computational economics, computational mechanics, computational fluid dynamics, computational science, computational electromagnetics, computational medicine, human computation, and computational chemistry.

Computational chemistry (CC) is part of the general area of computational science. It refers to using computers to model, simulate, and solve chemical problems. It can also be described as computational methods aimed at understanding molecules and materials.

The term theoretical chemistry may be regarded as the mathematical description of chemistry, whereas computational chemistry can be described as developing mathematical methods to the extent that results can be automated for implementation on a digital computer [1]. Computational chemistry should not be confused with computer science, although professionals in the two fields often collaborate. We must keep in mind that computers do not solve problems, humans do. Computers simply generate data.

Although chemists have been doing computations for ages, the field we refer to today as computational chemistry is a product of the digital age. With the development of digital computers in the 1940s, solutions of complex chemical systems became realizable. In the early 1950s, chemists began to use digital computers extensively. A brief history of early developments in CC is given in [2].

Computational chemistry has become a vital collaborator with experimental chemistry, whether in physical chemistry, organic chemistry, biochemistry, medicinal chemistry, or chromatography. It has attracted several Nobel Prize awards. Over the years, the Royal Swedish Academy of Sciences has awarded Nobel Prizes to chemists making groundbreaking contributions to computational chemistry. For example, three computational chemists, Paul Crutzen, Mario Molina, and F. Sherwood Rowland, won the Nobel Prize in Chemistry in 1995.

Computational chemistry is a rapidly developing branch of chemistry that applies computational methods to solve chemical problems. It is essentially the application of chemical, mathematical, and computing skills to chemical problems. It uses computers to generate information such as properties of molecules and materials.

It is a multidisciplinary field with applications in chemistry, biology, and materials science [3].

This chapter provides an introduction to computational chemistry. It begins with computational tools used by chemists, covers some applications, and concludes with comments.

8.2 COMPUTATIONAL TOOLS

Computational tools used by chemists include electronic structure methods, molecular dynamics simulations, cheminformatics (a field that combines laboratory data, chemical modeling, and information science methods), data analysis, visualization, and statistical analysis. As shown in Figure 8.1, modeling strategy requires a hierarchical scheme [4].

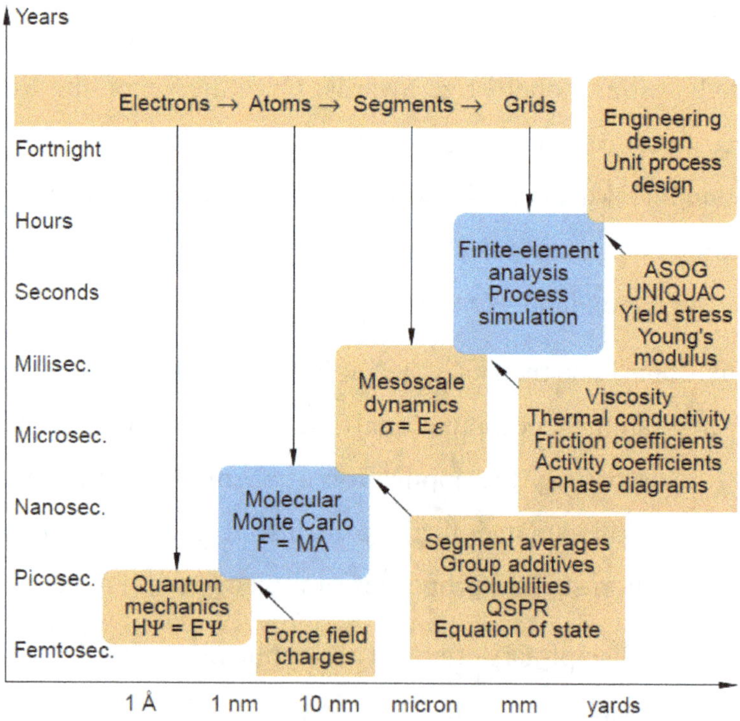

Figure 8.1 - Hierarchy of materials simulation [4].

Several self-sufficient computational chemistry software packages or programs exist today. These include Gaussian, GaussSum, GAMESS, GRAMPS, MOPAC, Spartan, Sybyl, AMBER, and Aces4. The programming languages used in developing these packages include FORTRAN, C, C++, and Python. Several commercial software manufacturers market a variety of products, and these are increasingly used in education. Computational chemists may freely choose from this wide range of packages. Unfortunately, most are proprietary and not interoperable [5].

8.3 APPLICATIONS

Computational chemistry is used to study the fundamental properties of atoms and molecules using quantum mechanics and thermodynamics. It can also be applied to solid-state problems. It influences our understanding of the way the world works and helps manufacturers design more productive and efficient processes. It can aid in the design of new materials and improve manufacturing efficiency and material performance. Combustion is another area where the computational approach has been especially useful.

The application of computational chemistry to carotenoids has gained attention in the last two decades. Its use in drug design has become standard practice, although the field's role in drug design is experiencing fundamental changes [4].

8.4 CONCLUSION

Computational chemistry has come of age. It has become an essential tool for chemists. Rapid advances in hardware and software have propelled CC into a strategic tool for productivity. Calculations with efficient parallel implementation, approaching the petascale level, are now possible. Such computations would be impossible without massively parallel supercomputer technology. The impact of these advances will be broad and encompassing, because chemistry is central to diverse areas such as biological systems, the pharmaceutical industry, and chemical manufacturing [6].

Because computational chemistry is integral to chemistry research, chemistry education should reflect this. It is both prudent and imperative that students in modern undergraduate curricula become accustomed to performing basic calculations using computational software packages. They should use computational chemistry to deepen their understanding of experimental work throughout the curriculum [7]. The pharmaceutical industry is a major employer of computational chemists.

Computational knowledge is transmitted from one researcher to another through conferences and journals. The Journal of Computational Chemistry publishes research on all aspects of the numerical solution of chemical problems.

REFERENCES

[1] "Computational chemistry."

https://en.wikipedia.org/wiki/Computational_chemistry

[2] H. S. Rzepa, "The Internet as a computational chemistry tool," Journal of Molecular Structure (Theochem), vol. 398–399, 1997, pp. 27–33.

[3] M. N. O. Sadiku, S. M. Musa, and O. M. Musa, "Computational chemistry," Computational Chemistry, vol. 110, 2017, pp. 48184–48185.

[4] S. Dasgupta, "The role and challenges of computational chemistry in industrial problems," Computing in Science & Engineering, Nov./Dec. 2000, pp. 52–60.

[5] N. M. O'Boyle, A. L. Tenderholt, and K. M. Langner, "Software news and updates: cclib – A library for package-independent computational chemistry algorithms," Journal of Computational Chemistry, vol. 29, no. 5, 2007, pp. 839–845.

[6] D. G. Truhlar and V. McKoy, "Computational chemistry," Computing in Science & Engineering, Nov./Dec. 2000, pp. 19–21.

[7] Z. L. Gasyna and S. A. Rice, "Computational chemistry in the undergraduate chemistry curriculum: Development of a comprehensive source formula," Journal of Chemical Education, vol. 76, no. 7, July 1999, pp. 1023–1029.

[8] N. H. Martin, "Integration of computational chemistry into the chemistry curriculum," Journal of Chemical Education, vol. 75, no. 2, Feb. 1998, pp. 241–243.

CHAPTER 9

COMPUTATIONAL SCIENCE

"Science is the most durable and nondivisive way of thinking about the human circumstance. It transcends cultural, national, and political boundaries. You don't have American science versus Canadian science versus Japanese science."

– Sam Harris

9.1 INTRODUCTION

Since the invention of the digital computer, its potential to aid scientific investigation has been well recognized. Computers are indispensable tools in solving complex problems in every sector, from traditional science and engineering domains to such key areas as finance, national security, medicine, and public health. Computers have advanced tremendously within just a few decades.

Computational science (CS) refers to the application of computer simulation to solve problems in various scientific disciplines. It is commonly regarded as the third pillar of scientific investigation, complementing theoretical analysis and laboratory experiments. The triad of theory, experiment, and computation is shown in Figure 9.1 [1].

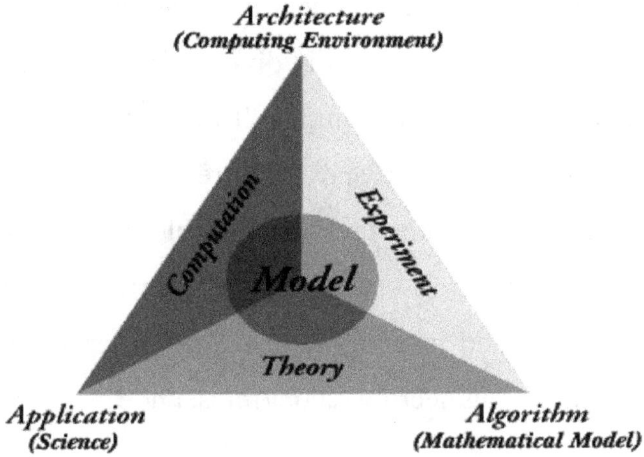

Figure 9.1 - Triad of theory, computation, and experiment [1].

CS provides the means of solving problems that are either mathematically intractable or inaccessible to traditional experimentation. Sometimes computation involves massive amounts of calculations and is implemented on high-performance computers or supercomputers [2]. Some areas of CS utilize large databases and require terabytes of storage, while others may require networks of computers. Software and programming are also important in computational science: FORTRAN, C++, Java, CORBA, MATLAB, Linux, Python, etc.

A computational scientist is usually a scientist, engineer, or applied mathematician who is skilled in scientific computing, programming languages, operating systems, visualization software, and parallel computing. Common numerical techniques used by computational scientists include finite elements, moment methods, finite difference methods, Monte Carlo methods, methods of integration, and the method of lines.

Computational science refers to the use of computer hardware and software to solve scientific problems in diverse areas such as science, engineering, finance, and the humanities. It lies at the intersection of mathematics, computer science, and the core disciplines of science and engineering. It has become an indispensable partner along with theory and experiment and is crucial to the security and welfare of nations. It is now applied in many investigations across chemistry, physics, mathematics, engineering, economics, and finance [3].

This chapter provides an introduction to computational science. It begins with applications, highlights challenges, and concludes with comments.

9.2 APPLICATIONS

Many disciplines have undergone a computational turn in the past decades. This has produced subdisciplines such as computational biology, computational chemistry, computational physics, and computational finance.

- **Computational Biology:** This is the science of modeling biological systems. Computational techniques are revolutionizing biology. A major challenge here is to understand how gene regulation controls fundamental biological processes. Computational anatomy and medicine have greatly helped in the analysis of biological information. Computational tools are now in the hands of doctors treating patients with all kinds of illnesses.

- **Computational Chemistry:** Computational chemistry is a rapidly developing branch of chemistry that applies computational methods to solve chemical problems. It is essentially the application of chemical, mathematical, and computing skills to such problems. It uses computers to generate information such as properties of molecules and materials. Computational chemistry has become a vital collaborator with experimental chemistry, whether in physical chemistry, organic chemistry, biochemistry, medicinal chemistry, or chromatography. It is a multidisciplinary field with applications in chemistry, biology, and materials science. The use of computational chemistry in drug design has become standard practice [4].
- **Computational Physics:** Computers are playing an increasingly important role in the lives and education of physicists. Many areas in physics involve problems that cannot be treated exactly or analytically and must be solved numerically. Computational physics develops models of physical phenomena and deepens understanding. It applies numerical methods to solve physical problems and enables learning physics with computers. Depending on whether the researcher is a digital native or digital immigrant, programming languages used in computational physics include FORTRAN, C, C++, and Python [5].
- **Computational Finance:** Computational finance is an important aspect of modern commerce. It combines computing

power and statistical analysis with the principles of finance and investment management. While traditional finance deals with making transactions that range from stock trades to corporate acquisitions, computational finance is more concerned with algorithms, modeling, and the computer software that powers most of the modern financial world. Modeling is a central activity in computational finance, and researchers sometimes experiment with human participants [6].

- **Computational Social Science (CSS):** This academic discipline combines the traditional social sciences with computer science. CSS can span the five traditional social science disciplines: psychology, anthropology, economics, political science, and sociology. It is teamwork between computer scientists and social scientists. While social scientists provide research questions, data sources, and acquisition methods, computer scientists contribute mathematical models and computational tools. CSS uses computational methods and statistical tools to analyze and model social phenomena, social structures, and human behavior [7].

Other areas of application include computational sociology, computational economics, computational mechanics, computational fluid dynamics, computational electromagnetics, computational medicine, computational archaeology, computational materials science, computational engineering, computational forensics, computational geophysics, computational history, computational informatics, computational intelligence, computational law, computational linguistics, computational mathematics, computational neuroscience, computational pharmacology, computational anatomy, computational imaging, and computational statistics. The list continues to grow.

9.3 CHALLENGES

While computational science offers great value to society, it faces challenges. Some CS software is large and expensive to maintain. This has led some industries to develop internally written and maintained codes [8].

There are also some "unsolved problems" in computational science. These difficult problems are related to number theory, geometry, combinatorics, graph theory, linear algebra, and group theory [9].

Since CS is a multidisciplinary field, working across disciplines can be challenging. Communication may present difficulties among interdisciplinary teams, as each discipline has its own vocabulary [10].

9.4 CONCLUSION

Computational science complements theory and experiment. It is a fast-growing, interdisciplinary, and exciting field that uses advanced computing and data analysis to solve complex problems. Dramatic advances in software and hardware development during the past half-century suggest that computational efforts in the next half-century will surpass all imagination. By applying digital tools, researchers have begun to build models that can unravel complex physical mysteries.

Computational Science and Engineering (CSE) is a multidisciplinary area of study offered in some universities today at undergraduate and graduate levels [9,10]. It is a rapidly evolving field, distinct from pure computer science and computer engineering. The next generation of computational scientists should obtain competence in several disciplines.

More information about computational science can be obtained from books on CS and from two major journals exclusively devoted to it:

- *Journal of Computational Science*
- *The International Journal of Computational Science*

REFERENCES

[1] M. Kafatos, P. Becker, and Z. Boybeyi, "Computational sciences: at the intersection of science and engineering—Case study for academic and research programs," Turkish Journal of Electrical Engineering and Computer Sciences, vol. 14, no. 1, 2006, pp. 77–90.

[2] "Computational science," Wikipedia, the free encyclopedia.

Available: https://en.wikipedia.org/wiki/Computational_science

[3] M. N. O. Sadiku, K. G. Eze, and S. M. Musa, "Computational science," International Journal of Trend in Research and Development, vol. 6, no. 5, Sept.–Oct. 2019, pp. 31–34.

[4] M. N. O. Sadiku, S. M. Musa, and O. M. Musa, "Computational chemistry," Computational Chemistry, vol. 110, 2017, pp. 48184–48185.

[5] M. N. O. Sadiku, A. E. Shadare, and S. M. Musa, "Computational physics: an introduction," International Journal of Engineering Research, vol. 6, no. 9, Sept. 2017, pp. 427–428.

[6] M. N. O. Sadiku, S. M. Musa, and O. S. Musa, "Computational finance," International Journal of Trend in Research and Development, vol. 4, no. 5, Sept.–Oct. 2017, pp. 375–376.

[7] M. N. O. Sadiku, S. M. Musa, and O. S. Musa, "Computational social science," Invention Journal of Research Technology in Engineering and Management, vol. 1, no. 12, Sept. 2017, pp. 25–26.

[8] A. M. Heroux and G. Allen, Computational Science and Engineering Software Sustainability and Productivity (CSESSP)

Challenges Workshop Report. Arlington, VA: Networking and Information Technology Research and Development (NITRD), Sept. 2016.

Available:https://www.nitrd.gov/PUBS/CSESSPWorkshopReport.pdf

[9] S. Gao and K. H. Chen, “Unsolved problems in computational science: III—A special self-avoiding walk,” Proceedings of the International Conference on Computational Science and Computational Intelligence, 2016, pp. 1371–1374.

[10] L. Carter, R. Botts, and C. Crockett, “Computational science programs: the background research,” Proceedings of the Frontiers in Education Conference (FIE), 2012.

[11] O. Yasar and R. H. Landau, “Elements of computational science and engineering education,” SIAM Review, vol. 45, no. 4, 2003, pp. 787–805.

CHAPTER 10

COMPUTATIONAL MATHEMATICS

"No human investigation can claim to be scientific if it doesn't pass the test of mathematical proof."

– Leonard da Vinci

10.1 INTRODUCTION

Mathematics may be regarded as the manipulation of algebra that allows a solution to be found for a given problem. It permeates nearly all facets of life and is a necessary prerequisite for the vast majority of modern technologies. Computational mathematics emerged as a branch of applied mathematics in the early 1950s with the computational power of the first digital computers. The goal of computational mathematics is to develop algorithms that solve mathematical problems computationally (i.e., using computers). Specifically, any algorithm we develop should fulfill four primary properties [1]:

- **Accuracy:** An accurate algorithm returns a result that is numerically very close to the correct, or analytical, result.
- **Efficiency:** An efficient algorithm solves the mathematical problem quickly with reasonable computational resources.
- **Robustness:** A robust algorithm works for a wide variety of inputs.

- **Stability:** A stable algorithm is not sensitive to small changes in the input.

Computational mathematics is concerned with the study of algorithms (or numerical methods) for solving computational problems in science, engineering, economics, finance, and other fields. Research areas in computational mathematics cover a broad spectrum, including differential equations, inverse problems, optimization, nonlinear dynamics, computational biology, numerical analysis, fluid mechanics, materials science, computational electromagnetics, acoustics, statistics, signal and image processing, probability theory and stochastic analysis, dynamical systems, and geometric mechanics [2]. Figure 10.1 shows a group in computational mathematics at the University of Oslo [3].

Figure 10.1 - A group in computational mathematics [3].

Mathematics is an indispensable tool for the efficient treatment of complex real-world problems arising from engineering, computer science, economics, finance, and more. Besides being a science in its own right, mathematics plays a fundamental role in the quantitative areas of nearly all academic disciplines, particularly in the natural sciences, engineering, business, finance, economics, and medicine. Computational mathematics blends computer science with applied mathematics. As a branch of applied mathematics, it is widely applicable [4].

This chapter provides a primer on computational mathematics. It begins with applications, discusses academic degrees, highlights benefits and challenges, and concludes with comments.

10.2 APPLICATIONS OF COMPUTATIONAL MATHEMATICS

Computational mathematics is a branch of applied mathematics devoted to the interaction between mathematics and computer computation. It is applicable to many fields where mathematics is essential, including the following [5]:

- **Engineering:** Computational mathematics is applied to solve technical problems.
- **Numerical Techniques:** Used in scientific computing and applied in areas such as algebra and equations. Computational mathematics designs and analyzes numerical algorithms and answers fundamental questions about the underlying physics. MATLAB, Mathematica, and Maple are common packages for numerical computation and graphics. Figure 10.2 displays a result from numerical analysis [6].

Figure 10.2 - Result from numerical analysis [6]

- **Computational Simulation:** Computer simulations are used across many fields. They involve solving mathematical problems computationally rather than analytically. Simulation is regarded as the third pillar of science, complementing theory and experiment. Applications include the virtual modeling of airplanes, satellites, automobiles, and ships. Tools include Monte Carlo methods, Markov chains, and queuing theory. Monte Carlo methods are especially used to introduce randomness. An example of computer simulation using MATLAB is shown in Figure 10.3 [7].

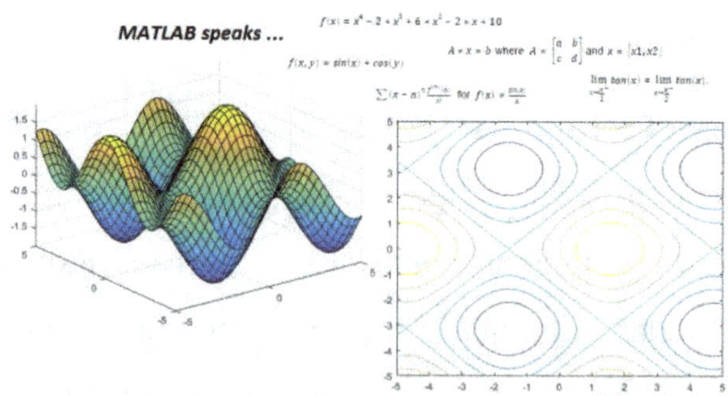

Figure 10.3 - An example of computer simulation using MATLAB [8].

- **Mathematical Models:** These express our understanding of the world. They are essential for interpreting the results of scientific experiments and for designing products, from airplanes to cell phones. Ordinary differential equations are often used to mathematically model problems in many fields. For example, mathematical economics applies models to economics, finance, and accounting.
- **Computational Linguistics:** The use of mathematical and computational methods in natural language analysis. Linguistics investigates the cognitive and social aspects of human language.
- **Social Sciences:** This modern scientific approach combines mathematical modeling with aspects of social science. Algorithms can be developed to simulate artificial societies, with subsequent analysis used to project social realities.
- **Financial Mathematics:** Applied mathematics is used to analyze and solve problems in financial markets. Informed market participants exploit opportunities to make a profit without risk of loss.

10.3 DEGREES IN COMPUTATIONAL MATHEMATICS

The degree in computational mathematics is usually offered by a department of mathematics. Programs emphasize the use of computers to solve mathematically modeled, real-world, data-driven problems. Some institutions also offer online programs. Students combine mathematical studies with applied fields, equipping them with both theory and computing skills. Graduates gain foundations in mathematics and computing (e.g., R, Python, SAS, MATLAB) to analyze data, draw conclusions, and pursue careers in academia, research, or industry.

1. Bachelor's Degree

The bachelor's program develops analytical and problem-solving skills in computing, mathematics, statistics, and science. It provides a strong foundation for applying mathematics across quantitative disciplines. Graduates find careers in banks, educational institutions, insurance companies, medical research, and stock markets.

The program's goals include [8]:

1. Develop problem-solving skills.
2. Develop inductive and deductive reasoning skills.
3. Understand the significance of central theorems and their applications.
4. Appreciate the precision and breadth of mathematical theories.
5. Foster abstract mathematical thinking.
6. Reason and compute with mathematical structures, conjecture and prove results, generalize, and analyze.
7. Apply general results to concrete situations.
8. Apply mathematical thinking to real-world problems.
9. Read, interpret, and generate mathematical proofs and examples.

10. Recognize the role of axiomatic systems and proofs in different branches (analysis, discrete mathematics, algebra, geometry).
11. Utilize technology, including computer algebra systems, to solve problems numerically, symbolically, and graphically.
12. Design and apply algorithms for numerical, algebraic, and graphical problems.
13. Build skills for lifelong learning in mathematics.
14. Build mathematical foundations for success in other disciplines.
15. Understand the principal concepts of calculus.
16. Develop conceptual understanding of sets and functions.
17. Acquire skills for careers in actuarial, financial, or related fields.
18. Prepare for careers in teaching by understanding mathematics profoundly and from multiple perspectives.
19. Communicate mathematics orally and in writing.
20. Gain familiarity with the history of mathematics.
21. Understand basic probability and statistics.
22. Prepare for graduate study in mathematics.
23. Prepare for non-teaching careers.

2. Master's Degree

The master's program prepares students for advanced industrial positions or doctoral studies. Students gain advanced skills in mathematics and simulation, with training in applied mathematics and a chosen area of application. Some programs offer thesis and non-thesis options [9].

Graduates will [10]:

- Gain in-demand skills for industries relying on modeling and simulation.
- Solve probability problems and analyze distribution functions.
- Apply statistical software confidently.
- Interpret and solve regression models.
- Understand the distinction between axioms, definitions, and theorems.
- Customize schedules with flexible learning formats.

Figure 10.4 shows graduate students specializing in computational mathematics at Swansea University [11].

Figure 10.4 - Some graduate students specializing in computational mathematics [11].

3. Doctoral Degree

Some mathematics departments offer interdisciplinary Ph.D. programs in computational mathematics. These focus on applied mathematics, numerical analysis, and scientific computation. Students receive training in computational fundamentals, conduct original research, and prepare for careers in academia, national labs, or industry. Application fields include fluid mechanics, materials science, mathematical biology, image processing, and mathematical finance [1].

Research priorities often include climate-ocean-atmosphere modeling, compressible flows, numerical methods for partial differential equations, and the application of AI and machine learning in these areas [12].

10.4 BENEFITS AND CHALLENGES

Computational mathematics involves mathematical research in areas of science and engineering where computing plays a central role. It is closely connected to many other mathematical branches and represents a major development in applied science. Training in computational mathematics is essential for careers in academia, national laboratories, and industry. Professionals in this field assist engineers, scientists, and managers in formulating complex problems and selecting appropriate methods and software.

The advanced principles and technologies of computational mathematics should be applied to global challenges. These principles enable the modeling of real-world phenomena using intelligent software and hardware platforms. Computational mathematics provides models to record, evaluate, and predict data. Its main limitations lie in human imagination and current levels of computer development, limitations likely to be overcome in time.

10.5 CONCLUSION

If you are seeking a career that draws on mathematics to solve problems in business, science, and engineering, you should consider a degree program in computational mathematics. Some programs are also offered online. You will explore core topics in computing structures, equations, and algorithms. Programs prepare students for 21st-century careers, expand knowledge in specialized fields, and address the shortage of skilled professionals in academia, industry, and national laboratories.

A fundamental change is taking place in computational mathematics. Areas such as machine learning, bioinformatics, network science, and medical imaging increasingly rely on computation and require new tractable methods.

More information about computational mathematics can be found in the books in [13–40] and the following related journals:

- *Applied and Computational Mathematics*
- *Advances in Computational Mathematics*
- *Advances in Computational Mathematics and Modelling*
- *Computational and Mathematical Methods*
- *Computational Mathematics and Mathematical Physics*

- *Computational Methods in Applied Mathematics*
- *Journal of Computational Mathematics*
- *Journal of Computational Mathematics and Data Science*
- *Journal of Applied and Computational Mathematics*
- *Journal of Advances in Applied & Computational Mathematics*
- *Journal of Mathematical Techniques and Computational Mathematics*
- *International Journal of Applied and Computational Mathematics*
- *International Journal of Pure and Computational Mathematics*

REFERENCES

[1] H. De Sterck and P. Ullrich, "Introduction to computational mathematics."
Available: https://climate.ucdavis.edu/AM341.pdf

[2] "Applied and computational mathematics."

Available: https://catalog.umd.umich.edu/graduate/college-arts-sciences-letters/applied-computational-mathematics/

[3] "Computational mathematics."

Available:https://www.mn.uio.no/math/english/research/groups/cm/

[4] M. N. O. Sadiku, U. C. Chukwu, and J. O. Sadiku, "Computational mathematics," Central Asian Journal of Mathematical Theory and Computer Sciences, vol. 4, no. 12, Dec. 2023, pp. 25–32.

[5] T. R. Nicely, "Computational mathematics: How it works?"

Available: https://www.trnicely.net/computational-mathematics/

[6] "Doctoral program in applied and computational mathematics."

Available:https://www.kth.se/en/sci/forskning/forskarutbildning/doktorsprogrammet-i-tillampad-matematik-och-berakningsmatematik-1.796276

[7] "Computational mathematics in symbolic math toolbox."

Available:https://www.mathworks.com/help/symbolic/computational mathematics-in-symbolic-math-toolbox.html

[8] "Computational mathematics, B.S."

Available:https://www.brooklyn.cuny.edu/web/academics/student-learning-outcomes/bs-computational-mathematics.php

[9] "Master of science in applied and computational mathematics."

Available: https://amath.washington.edu/master-science-applied-and-computational-mathematics

[10] "Applied and computational mathematics master's program online."

Available:https://ep.jhu.edu/programs/applied-and-computational-mathematics/

[11] "Masters degrees in computational mathematics." Available: https://www.findamasters.com/masters-degrees/computational-mathematics/

[12] "Ph.D. program in applied and computational mathematics." Available: https://www.icts.res.in/gsacm

[13] F. Cucker and J. M. Rojas, Foundations of Computational Mathematics: Proceedings of the SMALEFEST, Hong Kong. World Scientific, 2002.

[14] X. Yang, Introduction to Computational Mathematics, 2nd ed. World Scientific, 2015.

[15] J. E. Akin, Finite Elements for Analysis and Design: Computational Mathematics and Applications Series. Elsevier, 2014.

[16] V. I. Lebedev, An Introduction to Functional Analysis in Computational Mathematics. Springer, 1996.

[17] R. E. White, Computational Mathematics: Models, Methods, and Analysis with MATLAB and MPI. Chapman & Hall/CRC, 2003.

[18] W. E. Schiesser, Computational Mathematics in Engineering and Applied Science: ODEs, DAEs, and PDEs. Boca Raton, FL: CRC Press, 2014.

[19] J. W. Harris and H. Stöcker, Handbook of Mathematics and Computational Science. Springer, 1998.

[20] K. Schittkowski (ed.), Computational Mathematical Programming. Springer, 2013.

[21] L. Grattan (ed.), Computational Mathematics: Methods, Models and Analysis. Willford Press, 2020.

[22] A. Wigderson, Mathematics and Computation: A Theory Revolutionizing Technology and Science. Princeton University Press, 2019.

[23] B. P. Demidovich and I. A. Maron, Computational Mathematics. Central Books Ltd, 1987.

[24] B. Engquist (ed.), Encyclopedia of Applied and Computational Mathematics. Springer, 2015.

[25] R. C. Damaceanu, Applied Computational Mathematics in Social Sciences. Bentham Books, 2010.

[26] M. Mateos and P. Alonso, Computational Mathematics, Numerical Analysis and Applications. Springer, 2017.

[27] B. P. Demidovich and I. A. Maron, Computational Mathematics. Moscow: MIR Publishers, 2021.

[28] R. Devore, A. Iserles, and E. Suli (eds.), Foundations of Computational Mathematics (London Mathematical Society Lecture Note Series, No. 284). Cambridge University Press, 2001.

[29] D. S. Hooda and S. Kumar, Computational Mathematics and Information Technology. Narosa Publishing House, 2015.

[30] R. E. White, Computational Mathematics: Models, Methods, and Analysis with MATLAB® and MPI, 2nd ed. Chapman & Hall, 2016.

[31] W. Gautchi, Mathematics of Computation 1943–1993: A Half-Century of Computational Mathematics, Proceedings of Symposia in Applied Mathematics, 1995.

[32] P. G. Chareton (ed.), Computational Mathematics: Theory, Methods and Applications (Computational Mathematics and Analysis). Nova Science Publishers, UK ed., 2011.

[33] D. Mitsotakis, Computational Mathematics: An Introduction to Numerical Analysis and Scientific Computing with Python. Chapman & Hall, 2023.

[34] N. J. Daras and T. M. Rassias (eds.), Computational Mathematics and Variational Analysis (Springer Optimization and Its Applications, No. 159). Springer, 2020.

[35] A. Misra, Recent Trends in Computational Mathematics. New Century Publication, 2021.

[36] R. K. Brylinski and G. Chen (eds.), Mathematics of Quantum Computation. Boca Raton, FL: CRC Press, 2002.

[37] W. E. Schiesser, Computational Mathematics in Engineering and Applied Science: ODEs, DAEs, and PDEs. Boca Raton, FL: CRC Press, 2014.

[38] A. Toselli and O. Widlund, Domain Decomposition Methods—Algorithms and Theory. Springer, 2004.

[39] Z. Chen et al. (eds.), Advances in Computational Mathematics. Boca Raton, FL: CRC Press, 1998.

[40] P. Zimmermann et al., Computational Mathematics with SageMath. Society for Industrial and Applied Mathematics, 2018.

Part C: Social Sciences

CHAPTER 11

COMPUTATIONAL SOCIAL SCIENCE

"Look deep into nature, and then you will understand everything better."

– Albert Einstein

11.1 INTRODUCTION

The ongoing worldwide computerization has created new opportunities for researchers. The increasingly powerful instruments of computation have attracted considerable interest from researchers in relevant fields. Computing technologies such as data mining, machine learning, and statistics have been developed. The growth of this field has created new scientific disciplines such as computational biology, computational chemistry, computational economics, computational electrodynamics, computational electromagnetics, computational finance, computational fluid dynamics, computational geophysics, computational mechanics, computational physics, computational science, computational mathematics, computational sociology, and computational statistics [1].

Computational social science (CSS) can span all five traditional social science disciplines: psychology, anthropology, economics, political science, and sociology. It is the work of teams of computer scientists and social scientists. CSS is a multidisciplinary field that includes computational economics, computational sociology, distributed algorithms, statistics, machine learning, data mining, and several substantive social science fields. These include sociology, economics, psychology, political science, and marketing. Computational social scientists develop tools that enable the study of how humans think, feel, or behave in social situations (psychology), relate to each other (sociology), govern themselves (political science), handle wealth (economics), and create culture (anthropology) [2].

CSS combines the traditional social sciences with computer science. While social scientists provide research questions, data sources, and acquisition methods, computer scientists contribute mathematical models and computational tools. CSS uses computational methods and statistical tools to analyze and model social phenomena, social structures, and human social behavior [3].

This chapter begins with applications of computational social science, then presents its issues and challenges. The final section concludes with comments.

11.2 APPLICATIONS

Computational social science provides tools to process the vast amount of data emanating from social networking websites. It is being developed in organizations such as Google, Yahoo, and the National Security Agency.

CSS includes five core techniques: automated information extraction, geospatial analysis, complexity modeling, social simulation models, and social network analysis [4]. One reason human societies are complex is that there are numerous non-linear interactions between people. Society emerges from constant, dynamic change.

Agent-based simulations and models are developed by social scientists to explore social behavior and economic systems. These models are a form of mathematical model written in computer code. Early programming frameworks used languages such as FORTRAN, BASIC, Pascal, and C. Recent efforts employ C++, Java, and Python [5]. Social scientists also use computing and informatics to explore human-computer interaction. Anthropologists are using CSS methods to model social dynamics, test anthropological theory, and inform policy.

Social networks are an important focus of the social sciences. The data in such networks can be massive and unstructured, requiring big data architecture and funneling methods to manage. Such data include pictures, online purchases, and mobile transactions. The era of big data has transformed how researchers study social phenomena [6,7].

11.3 ISSUES AND CHALLENGES

Although CSS can provide great benefits, it also presents challenges, risks, and potential for abuse by governments and private entities. Without addressing these ethical issues and obstacles, advancements in CSS may put the public at risk.

Understanding CSS in both of its forms within the IC is an important contemporary challenge. In social and economic interactions, conflicts may arise. For example, the Internet has enabled the presence of hate and extremist groups. CSS requires technical skills beyond the traditional confines of social science and often requires collaboration with computer scientists. (For example, social scientists must be trained to handle big data.) Such interdisciplinary efforts are often challenging due to the different backgrounds of the researchers involved.

CSS models are usually developed by highly specialized multidisciplinary teams of experts and may take months to complete. This slow process may not reflect the dynamic nature of social spaces. Crowdsourced modeling may be a solution [8].

The vast quantities of data used for CSS analysis today are mainly controlled by businesses and governments. CSS may enable surveillance, profiling, and targeting of individuals. The potential damage from inappropriate disclosure of information is evident. As CSS develops, issues concerning methodology and ethics must be considered. Ethics addresses how information is accessed and how it is used. Guidelines and regulations must establish limits on the collection, retention, use, and disclosure of sensitive personal information [9].

CSS raises unavoidable questions about the privacy and politics of data science research, particularly in government and private-sector applications. The privacy issue must be addressed by developing technologies that protect privacy while preserving essential research data.

11.4 CONCLUSION

Computational social science is a practice-oriented discipline, where theoretical concerns have often been pushed to the background. The emergence of data-driven CSS has been gradual, mainly spearheaded by computer scientists and social scientists. Powerful computer simulations have been a particular boon to the field. CSS, with its focus on large-scale and social media data, offers great opportunities but also serious research challenges. Its potential value is gaining attention across multiple disciplines.

To meet the need for computational social scientists, courses and degrees are being offered at various universities. Graduate students are typically required to have a background in social sciences, computer science, engineering, or a related discipline. Additional information on CSS can be found in books available on Amazon.com.

REFERENCES

[1] R. C. Damaceanu, *Applied Computational Mathematics in Social Sciences*. Sharjah, United Arab Emirates: Bentham Science Publishers, 2010.

[2] M. Strohmaier and C. Wagner, “Computational social science for the World Wide Web,” *IEEE Intelligent Systems*, vol. 29, no. 5, pp. 84–88, Sept.–Oct. 2014.

[3] M. N. O. Sadiku, S. M. Musa, and O. S. Musa, “Computational social science,” *Invention Journal of Research Technology in Engineering and Management*, vol. 1, no. 12, pp. 25–26, Sept. 2017.

[4] B. F. Welles and I. Meirelles, “Visualizing computational social science: The multiple lives of a complex image,” *Science Communication*, vol. 37, no. 1, pp. 34–58, 2014.

[5] L. A. Kuznar, “High-fidelity computational social science in anthropology: Prospects for developing a comparative framework,” *Social Science Computer Review*, vol. 24, no. 1, pp. 15–29, Spring 2006.

[6] E. Ch’ng, “The value of using big data technologies in computational social science,” in *Proc. 2014 Int. Conf. Big Data Science and Computing*, Beijing, China, Aug. 2014.

[7] R. M. Chang, R. J. Kauffman, and Y. Kwon, “Understanding the paradigm shift to computational social science in the presence of big data,” *Decision Support Systems*, vol. 63, pp. 67–80, 2014.

[8] A. Ruvinsky and A. Roberts, "Building computational social science models from crowd insight," in *Proc. IEEE Int. Conf. Multimedia and Expo Workshops (ICMEW)*, Oct. 2013.

[9] A. Oboler, K. Welsh, and L. Cruz, "The danger of big data: Social media as computational social science," *First Monday: Peer-Reviewed Journal on the Internet*, vol. 17, no. 7, July 2012.

CHAPTER 12

COMPUTATIONAL ART

"You were born an original. Don't die a copy."

– John Mason

12.1 INTRODUCTION

Advances in computing are revolutionizing our understanding of nearly every aspect of human life. A few decades ago, art was considered an exclusively human skill, inaccessible to machines.

Figure 12.1 - A popular old art of Mona Lisa [2].

Today, however, artificial intelligence (AI) and sophisticated software are capable of writing poetry, composing music, and creating visual artworks. This has forced us to reconsider whether creativity is still the sole domain of humanity.

Figure 12.2 - Recent examples of computational arts [3].

Computational art represents the intersection of technology and culture. It encompasses artistic practices that rely on computation for their realization, whether through simulation of creative behavior, algorithmic processes, or machine collaboration. From music and architecture to fine arts and literature, computers are playing increasingly significant roles in creative activities [1].

This chapter introduces computational art. It discusses key applications, surveys academic degrees in the field, highlights its benefits, and concludes with reflections on its future.

12.2 APPLICATIONS OF COMPUTATIONAL ART

Computational art manifests in a wide range of practices, including the following:

- **Pattern Generation:** Uses computer-generated number sequences to produce intricate visual designs. Finite automata can translate binary sequences (0s and 1s) into drawing instructions, generating diverse artistic patterns [5].
- **Artist Robots:** Robots and AI software can compose music and reinterpret visual imagery using image recognition and stylistic filters. Technology giants, including Google, have pioneered art-robotics initiatives [6].

Figure 12.3 - Artist robot based on artificial intelligence [6].

- **Computational Photography:** Employs digital image capture and processing techniques that extend beyond traditional optics. Applications include panoramic stitching, high-dynamic-range (HDR) imaging, and light field cameras. Computational photography enables amateurs to produce professional-quality results [7][8][9].

Figure 12.5 - A typical computational art setup [9].

- **Algorithmic Art:** Visual or multimedia art generated through algorithms. Artists (sometimes called *algorists*) design code, functions, or processes that govern the creative output. Works may be displayed digitally or physically [10].

Figure 12.6 - An example of algorithmic art

[https://www.transfernow.net/dl/20250930zHYfdztl].

- **Computational Aesthetics:** Explores how computation itself drives new aesthetic experiences. Rather than being limited to form, computational aesthetics emphasizes processes, behaviors, and interaction, often producing artworks that invite subjective engagement [11].
- **Computational Drawing:** Uses programming as a medium for drawing, combining historical practices of drafting with modern computational tools [12].
- **Architectural Computation:** Integrates advanced digital design and programming into architecture. Students and practitioners create generative, responsive forms using tools like AI, parametric modeling, and coding environments [13].

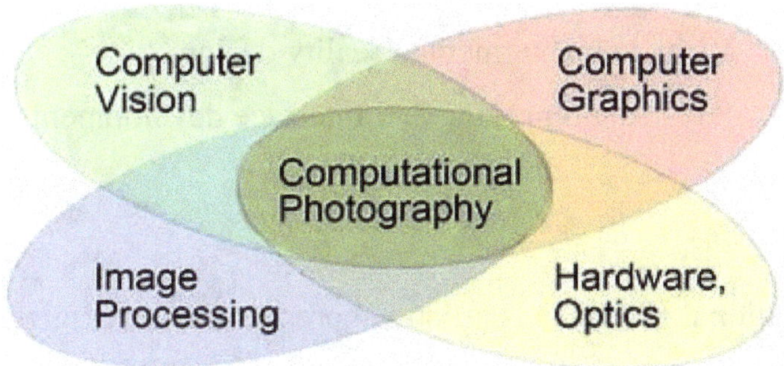

Figure 12.4 - The technologies comprising computation art [7].

12.3 DEGREES IN COMPUTATIONAL ART

Educational programs in computational art blend art, design, and computer science. They are typically offered at the **bachelor's** and **master's** levels.

- **Bachelor's Degree:** Students explore the intersection of design, art, and technology while learning programming as an artistic tool. Facilities often include high-end studios, VR systems, 3D printers, and exhibition opportunities. Graduates are prepared for roles in digital industries, creative practice, or entrepreneurship [14].
- **Master's Degree (MA in Computational Art):** Designed for graduate students across the arts and humanities, the program emphasizes both theory and practice. Students learn languages such as Python and C++, and work with platforms like Processing and Arduino. Coursework may include [15][16]:
    - Data-driven analysis and visualization
    - Interactive publishing and storytelling
    - Generative text, music, and visual systems
    - Virtual and augmented reality design
    - Physical computing and interface development

12.4 BENEFITS

Computational art expands artistic expression by leveraging AI and machine learning. Style-transfer techniques, for example, allow computers to mimic established artists or generate entirely new aesthetics [17].

Artists working in this field contribute to innovation by:

- Integrating computational technologies into emerging artistic applications.

- Promoting open access to tools, code, and collaborative platforms.
- Exploring socially relevant issues shaped by algorithms and data.

The result is a dynamic ecosystem where creativity and technology inform one another.

12.5 CONCLUSION

Computational art represents one of the most exciting intersections of technology and culture. From galleries to online platforms, artists, curators, and technologists are embracing computation as both a medium and a method. Artificial intelligence and machine learning are poised to become central to the next wave of creative practices.

Students trained in computational art develop conceptually provocative, technically innovative, and aesthetically engaging work. Graduates redefine the future of creativity by integrating artistic vision with computational fluency.

For further reading, see [1], [12], [18]–[22].

REFERENCES

[1] "Artificial intelligence and the arts: Toward computational creativity," https://www.bbvaopenmind.com/en/articles/artificial-intelligence-and-the-arts-toward-computational-creativity/

[2] "Mona Lisa – Leonardo da Vinci," Fine Art America, https://fineartamerica.com/featured/14-mona-lisa-leonardo-da-vinci.html?product=framed-print

[3] "Recent examples of computational arts," ResearchGate, https://www.researchgate.net/figure/Recent-examples-of-computational-arts_fig1_356564616

[4] M. N. O. Sadiku, C. M. M. Kotteti, and J. O. Sadiku, "Computational art," *International Journal of Trend in Research and Development*, vol. 10, no. 6, Nov.–Dec. 2023, pp. 220–223.

[5] S. Hollos and J. R. Hollos, *Pattern Generation for Computational Art*. Abrazol Publishing, 2013.

[6] "What is computational art? Can machines create art?" https://www.iberdrola.com/culture/computational-creativity-robot-art

[7] "Computational photography group," https://cphoto.fit.vutbr.cz/wp-content/uploads/2014/10/cphoto-1024x489.png

[8] “Computational photography,” *Wikipedia, the free encyclopedia*

https://en.wikipedia.org/wiki/Computational_photography

[9] “Computational photography,” NHK,

https://www.nhk.or.jp/strl/english/open2021/tenji/img/11_1.jpg

[10] “Algorithmic art,” *Wikipedia, the free encyclopedia*

https://en.wikipedia.org/wiki/Algorithmic_art

[11] M. Carvalhais and R. Lee, “Spectral and procedural creativity: A perspective from computational art,” *Transformations*, vol. 36, 2022, pp. 71–81.

[12] C. Lostritto, *Computational Drawing: From Foundational Exercises to Theories of Representation*. Applied Research & Design, 2019.

[13] “Architectural computation MSc,” University College London,
https://www.ucl.ac.uk/bartlett/architecture/programmes/postgraduate/architectural-computation-msc

[14] “BA (Hons) Fine Art: Computational Arts,” University of the Arts London,

https://www.arts.ac.uk/subjects/fine-art/undergraduate/ba-hons-fine-art-computational-arts-camberwell

[15] “MA Computational Arts,” Goldsmiths, University of London,

https://www.gold.ac.uk/pg/ma-computational-arts/

[16] "Master's Program in Computational Media, Arts & Cultures," Duke University, https://cmac.duke.edu/ma

[17] H. Uretmen, "Exploration: Computational art," Payette, June 2021,

https://www.payette.com/cool-stuff/exploration-computational-art/

[18] I. Greenberg, *Processing: Creative Coding and Computational Art*. Berkeley, CA: Apress, 2007.

[19] R. Melnik (ed.), *Mathematical and Computational Modeling: With Applications in Natural and Social Sciences, Engineering, and the Arts*. John Wiley & Sons, 2015.

[20] G. Levin and T. Brain, *Code as Creative Medium: A Handbook for Computational Art and Design*. MIT Press, 2021.

[21] M. Carvalhais, *Art and Computation*. V2, 2022.

[22] J. Braman, G. Vincenti, and G. Trajkovski, *Handbook of Research on Computational Arts and Creative Informatics*. Information Science Reference, 2009.

CHAPTER 13

COMPUTATIONAL INTELLIGENCE

"The measure of intelligence is the ability to change."

– Albert Einstein

13.1 INTRODUCTION

Computational intelligence (CI) refers to recreating human-like intelligence in a computing machine. It consists of a set of computing systems with the ability to learn and deal with new situations such that the systems are perceived to have some attributes of intelligence. CI techniques are computational systems that try to mimic human behavior, such as perception, reasoning, learning, evolution, and adaptation. It is concerned with discovery of structures in data and recognition of patterns. It involves using an algorithm to capture hidden knowledge from data and use it to train an "intelligent machine" to make complex decisions without human intervention [1]. It encompasses techniques such as neural networks, fuzzy logic, and evolutionary computation which derive rules, patterns, and develop complex mappings from data.

The concept of computational intelligence (soft computing) was first used in 1990 by the IEEE Neural Networks Council, which later became the IEEE Computational Intelligence Society. CI provides knowledge engineers with a set of robust techniques and intelligent tools for various applications. CI methods provide the ability to learn from experience and extract knowledge.

Some consider CI as a branch of AI, while others consider them as parallel disciplines. Although Artificial Intelligence (AI) and Computational Intelligence (CI) seek a similar long-term goal, they are different. While AI is based on hard computing methods, CI is based on soft computing methods, which enable adaptation to many situations. One may regard AI as human-based, and CI as nature-based [2].

This chapter provides an introduction to computational intelligence (CI). It begins with discussing what computational intelligence is all about. It addresses common computational intelligence techniques. It presents some typical applications of CI. It highlights the main benefits and challenges of CI. The last section concludes with comments.

13.2 WHAT IS COMPUTATIONAL INTELLIGENCE?

Computational intelligence (CI) refers to the ability of a computer to learn a specific task from experimental observation. It is an emerging discipline which provides powerful tools for modeling and analyzing complex systems. Some regard CI as a branch of artificial intelligence that comprises algorithms inspired by nature to address complex real-world problems. CI is the study of the design of intelligent systems. A system is regarded as "intelligent" only if it satisfies learning and decision-making requirements. The best-known manifestation of intelligence is human intelligence. The characteristic of "intelligence" is usually attributed to humans so that CI is a way of performing like human beings and using human-like reasoning, i.e., it uses inexact and fuzzy knowledge. Thus the goal of CI is to recreate human-like intelligence in a human-made machine.

The term "Artificial Intelligence" was coined by John McCarthy in 1956. The concept of "Computational Intelligence" was popularized in the 1990s by the IEEE Neural Networks Council. CI consists of a set of heuristics which exhibit intelligence such as learning, improvement through learning, flexibility, and adaptation. The ongoing worldwide computerization has created new opportunities for researchers. All branches of science and art have become computational: computational biology, computational physics, computational chemistry, computational ecology, computational linguistics, computational electromagnetics, computational finance, computational mechanics, computational social science, computational epistemology, computational intelligence, and so on. Computational intelligence is known for including powerful techniques such as artificial neural networks, fuzzy systems, evolutionary computation, learning theory, or probabilistic methods.

Although Artificial Intelligence (AI) and Computational Intelligence (CI) seek a similar goal of developing intelligent machines, they are different. AI is based on hard computing techniques, while CI is based on soft computing methods. AI operates in a top-down manner, while CI operates in a bottom-up manner. Some regard CI to be a subset or branch of AI [3]. Some of the most successful AI systems are based on CI. Hard (traditional) computing emphasizes precision, certainty, and rigor, while soft computing requires that computation, reasoning, and decision making exploit the tolerance for imprecision and uncertainty wherever possible. Figure 13.1 illustrates hard and soft computing. The relationship between AI, CI, and soft computing is depicted in Figure 13.2.

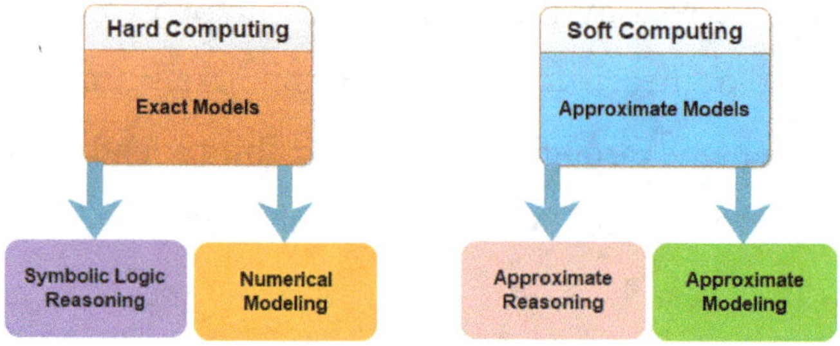

Figure 13.1 - Hard and soft computing.

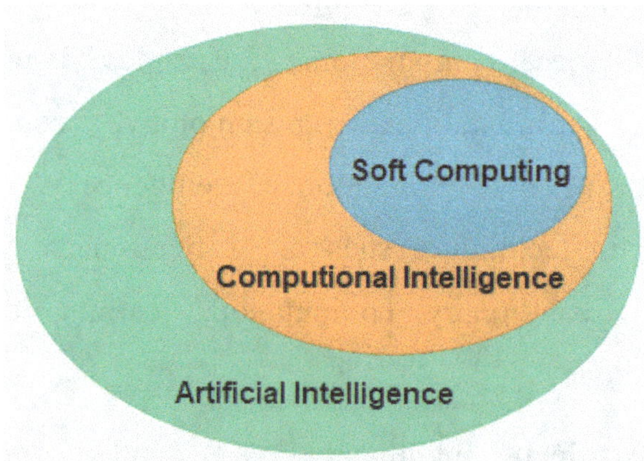

Figure 13.2 - Relationship between AI, CI, and soft computing.

13.3 COMPUTATIONAL INTELLIGENCE TECHNIQUES

CI approaches aim at creating intelligent systems by using innovative and nature-inspired algorithms. Traditionally, CI uses a combination of five main complementary techniques: Neural Networks, Fuzzy Systems, Evolutionary Computation, Genetic Algorithm, and Probabilistic Reasoning. Some of these CI techniques have their origins in biological systems and are shown in Figure 13.3. They are briefly explained as follows [4–7]:

- **Neural Networks:** These are the most popular artificial learning tools. Artificial neural network (ANN) is a CI method that mimics the neural system of the human brain. NNs are parallel distributed networks that have the ability to learn and generalize from examples. NNs include feedforward NNs, recurrent NNs, self-organizing NNs, deep learning, and convolutional neural networks. An NN architecture typically consists of an input layer, one or more hidden layers, and an output layer. With large numbers of input variables, it can be difficult for the user to understand the logic represented in this mapping of inputs to output. A typical structure of ANN is shown in Figure 13.4.
- **Fuzzy Systems:** Fuzziness refers to the inexact or imprecise nature of common terms. It constitutes a form of "approximate reasoning." This area of research includes fuzzy sets and systems, fuzzy clustering and classification, fuzzy controllers,

linguistic summarization, and fuzzy neural networks. Fuzzy algorithms attempt to capture the uncertainty and imprecision in rule-based representations that are not easily quantified by other methods.

- **Evolutionary Computation:** Evolutionary computation (EC) is a CI model used to mimic the biological evolution phenomenon. EC solves optimization problems by generating, evaluating, and modifying a population of possible solutions. EC currently includes five algorithms: genetic algorithm (GA), evolutionary programming (EP), evolution strategies (ES), genetic programming (GP), and swarm intelligence (SI). EC is very useful for optimizing the connections and weightings between the input layer, the hidden layer(s), and the output layers for an NN model.

- **Genetic Algorithm:** This is a subset of evolutionary computation. It takes all its inspiration from nature. The concept of genetic algorithm is to mimic natural selection in which the fittest elements are chosen.

- **Probabilistic Reasoning:** Probabilistic reasoning is often used in dealing with uncertain and incomplete data in artificial intelligence. The aim of probabilistic reasoning is to combine the capability of probability theory with the capability of deductive logic to exploit structure.

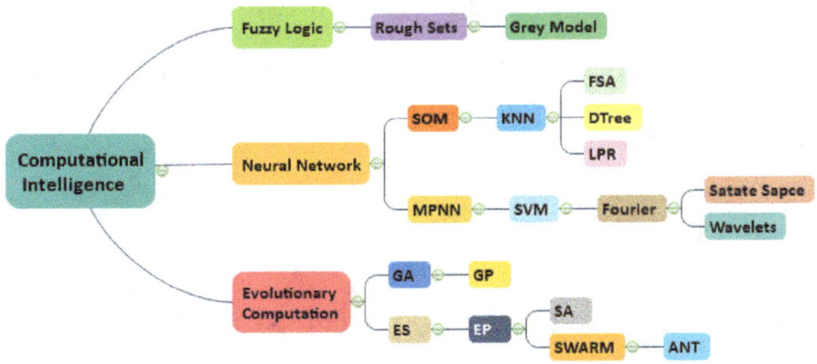

Fig. 13.3 - Computational intelligence techniques.

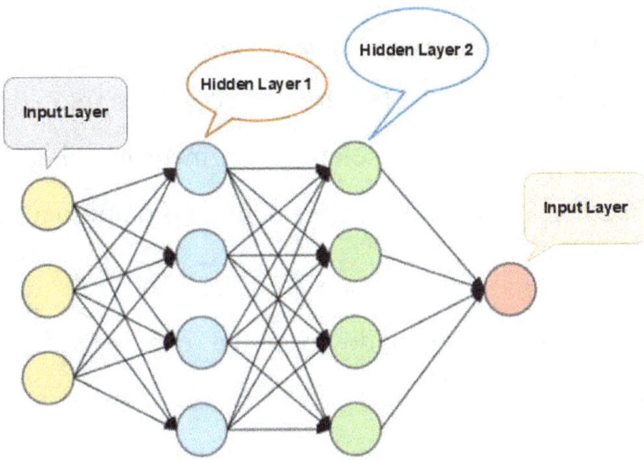

Figure 13.4 - Typical structure of ANN.

Today, these computing techniques are used in classification, regression, pattern recognition, medicine, system modeling, decision making, and food engineering. CI is an evolving field. In addition to the five main constituents, it encompasses computing paradigms like ambient intelligence, swarm intelligence, artificial immune systems, cultural learning, data mining, natural language processing, and artificial intelligence. The common characteristics of these techniques are their collective intelligence and adaptability to a changing environment. Due to their efficiency and simplicity, the algorithms have been employed successfully for problem solving across social and natural sciences [8].

13.4 APPLICATIONS

CI plays a major role in developing successful intelligent systems, including games and cognitive developmental systems. It provides solutions to complex real-world problems to which mathematical or traditional modeling does not perform well. Researchers have used CI techniques to design intelligent and context-aware algorithms to incorporate the aforementioned features. Successful applications of CI have been found in computer science, engineering, data analysis, business, marketing, medical, e-government, and manufacturing.

- **Wireless Sensor Networks (WSNs):** These are networks of distributed autonomous devices that can sense or monitor environmental conditions. WSNs face many challenges, mainly caused by communication failures, storage and computational constraints, and limited power supply. Computational intelligence has been successfully applied to address various challenges such as data aggregation and fusion, energy-aware routing, task scheduling, security, optimal deployment, and localization. CI provides adaptive mechanisms that exhibit intelligent behavior in complex and dynamic environments like WSNs [9].
- **Business:** CI techniques have been used to develop business intelligence and solve financial market problems. The

techniques have been applied to many areas in business such as marketing, e-commerce, financial management, decision making, classification, time series forecasting, and optimization [10]. CI simplifies the problem of predicting future financial markets.

- **Finance and Economics:** The financial sector is crucial to the economic and social organization of modern society. The number of applications of CI in this area is huge and covers anything from asset pricing or game analysis to time series forecasting. The range of approaches that have already been used in economics and finance includes fuzzy systems, neural networks, evolutionary computation, support vector machines, and ant algorithms [11].
- **Control:** CI methodologies are currently applied to all areas of control. Applications of CI in control include neural network control, fuzzy control, reinforcement learning, and brain-machine interfaces. Neural networks have been successfully applied to system control with their universal approximation and adaptation capabilities [12].
- **Medicine:** CI models can analyze large amounts of data in order to predict healthcare outcomes for individual patients. They can handle the imprecision and uncertainty which is typically apparent in clinical and biological data. They are suitable for clinical predictions as they are efficient in finding patterns in data which contain noisy features, and which traditional statistical models alone often fail to handle [13].

Researchers have used various CI techniques for early diagnosis of heart disease and to improve diagnosis accuracy [14]. The application of CI can be either diagnostic or therapeutic [15]. Applying CI techniques in complex medical data can provide better management, faster performance, and higher accuracy.

- **Music Composition:** CI techniques such as neural networks, fuzzy systems, and evolutionary computation provide powerful tools for modeling, learning, and optimization. These techniques have been applied successfully to music composition, which involves musical elements such as timbre, pitch, rhythm, motive, phrase, and chord [16].
- **Social Creativity:** CI can be used to leverage social creativity. Creative solutions to complex problems faced by organizations come from joint thinking as opposed to traditional views of creativity that focus on the individual. CI can broaden group participation by linking groups with social networks and can facilitate divergent thinking and inspiration by linking users to large amounts of online information and social media [17].

Other applications of CI include production electronics, games, hydrology, drug discovery and development, HVAC systems, transfer learning, sports, bioinformatics, intrusion detection, information systems, biological systems, power systems (smart grid), oil and gas reservoir management, air pollution monitoring, manufacturing systems, corrosion damage assessments, coral reef ecosystems, environmental planning, logistics, and supply chain management. The combination of big data and computational intelligence provides a powerful tool. CI has the potential to influence modern societies, businesses, and the public [18].

13.5 BENEFITS

Computational intelligence is a set of nature-inspired computational techniques for addressing complex real-world problems for which traditional modeling does not perform well. It is efficient in solving problems which require reasoning and decision making. It produces more robust, simpler, and tractable solutions than traditional techniques. A long-term goal for CI is creating cognitive systems that could compete with humans in a large number of areas.

CI techniques can solve real-world complex problems in which traditional approaches are ineffective. They perform efficient approximations within reasonable computation time because they often use non-deterministic techniques. Nonlinear characteristics of optimization models and 3D problems pose challenges for traditional mathematical programming methods. CI techniques perform well in nonlinear optimization problems and allow modeling of systems with varying levels of complexity [19]. Other advantages of CI methods are that they often work efficiently, are fault-tolerant, and are well-suited for parallelization.

13.6 CHALLENGES

The biggest disadvantage of CI, compared to deterministic methods, is that the optimal solution(s) can generally be neither proved nor guaranteed to be found [20]. Attempts to combine different CI methods remain a challenge. Another major challenge facing CI approaches is the problem of extracting knowledge from data.

Each of the various CI techniques has some advantages and suffers from some disadvantages. Therefore, there is no solution methodology that is universally superior. Hybrid methods may generate better results than single methods.

Some believe that CI is a dead-end, unachievable attempt to recreate intelligence in a computing machine. This belief is based on the inconsistent and contradictory goal of CI—while "computational" implies data processing ability, "intelligence" implies the ability to process information [21].

There have also been issues like security and privacy in data analysis of sensitive information, particularly in medical applications. There are also challenges with big data procured from complex healthcare sources [22]. Some of the key issues facing computational intelligence are presented in Figure 13.5.

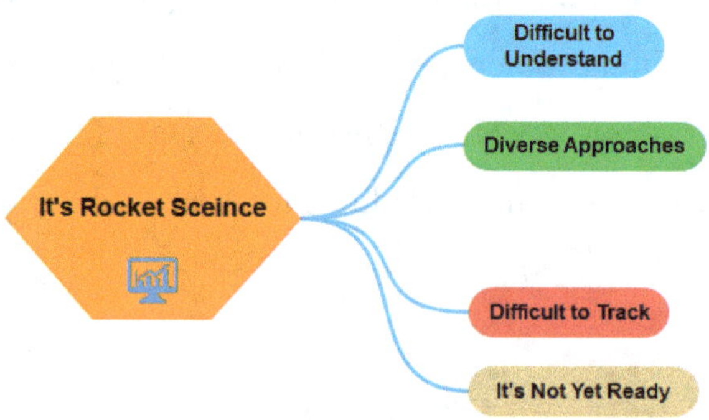

Figure 13.5 - Some key issues in computational intelligence.

13.7 CONCLUSION

Computational intelligence (CI) is a newly evolving research field in artificial intelligence. It uses various techniques such as artificial neural networks, evolutionary computation, fuzzy systems, support vector machines, deep learning, swarm intelligence, and hybrid methods. The major goal of researchers in CI is mimicking nature with artificial technologies. CI develops intelligent systems with the ability to learn, deal with new situations, and reason. It is giving birth to blended intelligence and web intelligence.

The growing interest in CI research can perhaps best be illustrated by the increasing number of journals, books, and articles published on CI in recent years. As more and more engineering applications use CI techniques, the need to train students in this area increases [23]. CI is yet to reach maturity as a discipline in its own right.

For more information on computational intelligence, see the books in [20,24–54] and several books on Amazon.com. A lot of information is also available in the following journals devoted to CI:

- Computational Intelligence
- Computational Intelligence: An International Journal
- Computational Intelligence and Neuroscience
- Applied Computational Intelligence and Soft Computing
- IEEE Transactions on Emerging Topics in Computational Intelligence

- IEEE Transactions on Computational Intelligence and AI in Games
- IEEE Computational Intelligence Magazine
- Journal of Computational Intelligence in Finance
- Journal of Computational Intelligence in Bioinformatics
- Journal of Advanced Computational Intelligence and Intelligent Informatics
- International Journal of Computational Intelligence Systems
- International Journal of Computational Intelligence and Applications
- International Journal of Computational Intelligence
- International Journal of Computational Intelligence and Organizations
- International Journal of Computational Intelligence Research
- International Journal of Computational Intelligence Theory and Practice

REFERENCES

[1] G. Casalino, "Computational intelligence for smart laser materials processing," *Optics and Laser Technology*, vol. 100, 2018, pp. 165–175.

[2] M. N. O. Sadiku, S. M. Musa, and O. M. Musa, "Computational intelligence: A primer," *International Journal of Advanced Engineering and Technology*, vol. 3, no. 4, Oct. 2019, pp. 34–36.

[3] M. N. O. Sadiku, J. Foreman, and S. M. Musa, "Computational intelligence," *European Scientific Journal*, vol. 14, no. 21, July 2018, pp. 56–60.

[4] "What is computational intelligence?"

https://cis.ieee.org/about/what-is-ci

[5] D. Hecht, "Applications of machine learning and computational intelligence to drug discovery and development," *Drug Development Research*, vol. 72, 2011, pp. 53–65.

[6] U. Kumari, "Soft computing applications: A perspective view," *Proceedings of the 2nd International Conference on Communication and Electronics Systems*, 2017, pp. 787–789.

[7] M. N. O. Sadiku, Y. Wang, S. Cui, and S. M. Musa, "Soft computing: An introduction," *International Journal of Advanced Research in Computer Science and Software Engineering*, vol. 8, no. 6, June 2018, pp. 63–65.

[8] I. Fister et al., "Computational intelligence in sports: Challenges and opportunities within a new research domain," *Applied Mathematics and Computation*, vol. 262, 2015, pp. 178–186.

[9] R. V. Kulkarni, A. Forster, and G. K. Venayagamoorthy, "Computational intelligence in wireless sensor networks: A survey," *IEEE Communications Surveys & Tutorials*, vol. 13, no. 1, First Quarter 2011, pp. 68–96.

[10] Y. F. Hernández-Julio et al., "Framework for the development of business intelligence using computational intelligence and service-oriented architecture," *Proceedings of the 12th Iberian Conference on Information Systems and Technologies (CISTI)*, 2017, pp. 1–7.

[11] P. Isasi et al., "Applied computational intelligence for finance and economics," *Computational Intelligence*, vol. 23, no. 2, 2007, pp. 111–116.

[12] A. E. Ruano, "Computational intelligence in control," *Proceedings of the 19th World Congress, The International Federation of Automatic Control*, Cape Town, South Africa, Aug. 2014, pp. 8867–8878.

[13] G. Cosma et al., "A survey on computational intelligence approaches for predictive modeling in prostate cancer," *Expert Systems with Applications*, vol. 70, 2017, pp. 1–19.

[14] M. A. Jabbar, B. L. Deekshatulu, and P. Chandra, "Computational intelligence technique for early diagnosis of heart disease," *Proceedings of IEEE International Conference on Engineering and Technology (ICETECH)*, Coimbatore, India, Mar. 2015.

[15] S. Wiwanitkit and V. Wiwanitkit, “Computational intelligence in tropical medicine,” *Asian Pacific Journal of Tropical Biomedicine*, vol. 6, no. 4, 2016, pp. 350–352.

[16] C. H. Liu and C. K. Ting, “Computational intelligence in music composition: A survey,” *IEEE Transactions on Emerging Topics in Computational Intelligence*, vol. 1, no. 1, Feb. 2017, pp. 2–15.

[17] D. Apostolou et al., “Facilitating creativity in collaborative work with computational intelligence software,” *IEEE Computational Intelligence Magazine*, May 2016, pp. 29–40.

[18] R. Iqbal et al., “Big data analytics: Computational intelligence techniques and application areas,” *Technological Forecasting and Social Change*, 2018.

[19] M. Li, “Application of computational intelligence in modeling and optimization of HVAC systems,” Master’s thesis, The University of Iowa, Dec. 2009.

[20] T. Hanne and R. Dornberger, *Computational Intelligence in Logistics and Supply Chain Management*. Springer, 2017, ch. 2.

[21] E. Diamant, “Computational intelligence: Are you crazy? Since when has intelligence become computational?” *Proceedings of IEEE Symposium Series on Computational Intelligence (SSCI)*, Dec. 2016.

[22] A. Kalantari et al., “Computational intelligence approaches for classification of medical data: State-of-the-art, future challenges and research directions,” *Neurocomputing*, 2017, pp. 1–21.

[23] M. Zhang, “Experience of teaching computational intelligence in an undergraduate level course,” *IEEE Computational Intelligence Magazine*, Aug. 2011, pp. 57–59.

[24] A. Konar, *Computational Intelligence: Principles, Techniques and Applications*. Springer, 2005.

[25] W. Pedrycz, *Computational Intelligence: An Introduction*. Boca Raton, FL: CRC Press, 1998.

[26] D. Poole, A. Mackworth, and R. Goebel, *Computational Intelligence – A Logical Approach*. Oxford University Press, New York, 1998.

[27] Z. Chen, *Computational Intelligence for Decision Support*. Boca Raton, FL: CRC Press, 2000.

[28] A. Kusiak, *Computational Intelligence in Design and Manufacturing*. Wiley-Interscience, 2000.

[29] D. Andina and D. T. Pham, *Computational Intelligence: For Engineering and Manufacturing*. Springer, 2007.

[30] A. T. Azar and S. Vaidyanathan, *Computational Intelligence Applications in Modeling and Control*. Springer, 2015.

[31] R. Kruse et al., *Computational Intelligence*. Springer, 2013.

[32] W. Pedrycz and S. M. Chen, *Information Granularity, Big Data, and Computational Intelligence*. Springer, 2014.

[33] A. Kordon, *Applying Computational Intelligence: How to Create Value*. Springer, 2010.

[34] N. Ansari and E. Hou, *Computational Intelligence for Optimization*. London, UK: Kluwer Academic Publishers, 1997.

[35] R. Srivastava et al. (eds.), *Computational Intelligence for Machine Learning and Healthcare Informatics*. De Gruyter, 2020.

[36] H. Deng et al. (eds.), *Artificial Intelligence and Computational Intelligence*. Springer, 2013.

[37] M. Gui et al., *Computational Intelligence and Soft Computing Applications in Healthcare Management Science*. IGI Global, 2020.

[38] C. Piñeiro et al. (eds.), *Trends in Mathematics and Computational Intelligence*. Springer, 2019.

[39] A. T. Azar and S. Vaidyanathan (eds.), *Computational Intelligence Applications in Modeling and Control*. Springer, 2015.

[40] R. C. Eberhart and Y. Shi, *Computational Intelligence: Concepts to Implementations*. Elsevier, 2013.

[41] R. Kruse et al., *Computational Intelligence: A Methodological Introduction*. 2nd ed. Springer, 2013.

[42] K. Suzuki (ed.), *Computational Intelligence in Biomedical Imaging*. Springer, 2014.

[43] P. P. Angelov, *Handbook on Computational Intelligence (in 2 Volumes)*. World Scientific, 2016.

[44] J. Kacprzyk and W. Pedrycz, *Springer Handbook on Computational Intelligence*. Springer, 2015.

[45] A. P. Engelbrecht, *Computational Intelligence: An Introduction*. 2nd ed. Wiley Publishing, 2007.

[46] A. Chatterjee and P. Siarry, *Computational Intelligence in Image Processing*. Springer, 2013.

[47] J. Fulcher and L. C. Jain (eds.), *Computational Intelligence: A Compendium*. Springer, 2008.

[48] K. Pancerz and E. Zaitseva (eds.), *Computational Intelligence, Medicine and Biology*. Springer, 2015.

[49] H. K. Lam, S. S. H. Ling, and H. T. Nguyen (eds.), *Computational Intelligence and Its Applications: Evolutionary Computation, Fuzzy Logic, Neural Network and Support Vector Machine Techniques*. London, UK: Imperial College Press, 2012.

[50] T. Islam et al. (eds.), *Computational Intelligence Techniques and Applications*. Springer, 2014.

[51] L. Jain and P. De Wilde (eds.), *Practical Applications of Computational Intelligence Techniques*. Springer, 2001.

[52] M. G. Negoita and B. Reusch (eds.), *Real World Applications of Computational Intelligence*. Springer, 2005.

[53] V. Palade and C. D. Bocaniala, *Computational Intelligence in Fault Diagnosis*. Springer, 2000.

[54] L. N. de Castro and J. Timmis, *Artificial Immune Systems: A New Computational Intelligence Approach*. Springer, 2002.

[55] L. Wang and X. Fu, *Data Mining with Computational Intelligence*. Springer, 2005.

CHAPTER 14

COMPUTATIONAL STATISTICS

"The best way to find yourself is to lose yourself in the service of others."

– Mahatma Gandhi

14.1 INTRODUCTION

Many disciplines have undergone a computational turn in the past decades. The recent computational turn has produced sub-disciplines such as computational biology, computational chemistry, computational physics, computational electromagnetics, computational mechanics, computational fluid dynamics, computational humanities, and computational finance. Computation plays a vital role in modern statistics.

Computational statistics (or statistical computing) is a branch of computational science (or mathematical sciences) that is focused on statistics. It is essentially what statisticians do with the computer. It helps in the numerical solution of statistical problems. It requires practitioners to master basic skills that will enable them to solve many problems which cannot be tackled using classical techniques [1].

Computational statistics (CS) appeals to both computer scientists and statisticians. On one hand, computer scientists need to use statistics in areas such as artificial intelligence, data mining, data compression, machine learning, and software quality. On the other hand, statisticians traditionally spend a large portion of their working time using computers. They need computing skills to analyze large amounts of data in a timely manner, to conduct data analysis with software, and to implement new statistical methods [2].

Popular software used in CS includes R, S-Plus, and MATLAB. R is a powerful system for statistical computation and graphics. S-Plus is a commercial implementation of the S object-oriented programming language. MATLAB has relevant toolboxes for computational statistics including the Statistics Toolbox, the Curve Fitting Toolbox, and the Spline Toolbox [3].

Since the advent of digital computers, the field of computational statistics has emerged as a distinct discipline. Computational statistics methods deal with the analysis and application of numerical methods to solve statistical problems. Statisticians have traditionally relied on numerical tools to analyze and interpret their data [4].

This chapter provides an introduction to computational statistics. It begins with applications of computational statistics, addresses challenges facing the field, and concludes with comments.

14.2 APPLICATIONS

Computational statistics technology is widely applied in several areas. These include the following [1]:

1. **Operational Research:** Application of scientific techniques to decision-making problems in industry. Solutions depend on numerical optimization and computational statistics.
2. **Stochastic Differential and Partial Differential Equations:** Numerical solutions are crucial across computational science

and engineering. These equations arise in areas such as physics, biology, and finance.

3. **Numerical Integration:** High-precision quadrature is found in many applications. Multi-dimensional integration is particularly challenging.
4. **Simulation Techniques:** Simulations are numerical experiments, often involving Monte Carlo and Markov Chain Monte Carlo (MCMC) methods.
5. **Monte Carlo Methods:** A versatile tool of computational statistics. They simulate random experiments to provide approximate solutions within statistical certainty, requiring a source of random numbers.
6. **Markov Chain Monte Carlo (MCMC):** A special class of Monte Carlo methods based on Markov processes, characterized by the memoryless property.
7. **Random Number Generation:** Central to Monte Carlo methods, simulation, and standard statistical approaches. Most use pseudorandom numbers, which are deterministic but appear random.
8. **Machine Learning:** Uses numerical algorithms from computational mathematics to extract patterns from data. It applies observational data to infer relationships based on hypotheses.

Other applications include optimization, education, preventive medicine, and warranty forecasting.

14.3 CHALLENGES

CS brings computational challenges since it inherently involves a large amount of computation. It includes statistical methods that are computationally intensive. A recent challenge is the extremely large scale of modern data. Analysis often requires massive computations, demanding high-performance computers.

One limitation in statistical analysis is the use of color in graphical displays [5]. Nonlinear formulations, while often more natural, are harder to solve. Ongoing challenges include increasing scale and complexity of data analysis applications.

14.4 CONCLUSIONS

Computational statistics is concerned with efficient methods of obtaining numerical solutions to statistically formulated problems. CS methods enable statistical analysis through computational techniques and processes. CS is evolving and growing in importance.

In modern academic programs, students preparing to work as statisticians must be grounded in computing instruction and CS techniques. Their preparation must have a strong computational component. Most students are exposed to SAS, S-Plus, and R [6].

Readers are encouraged to consult introductory texts and handbooks on the subject [5,7–11]. One should also consult the international journals devoted to CS:

- *Computational Statistics*
- *Computational Statistics & Data Analysis*
- *Journal of Computational and Graphical Statistics*
- *Journal of the Japanese Society of Computational Statistics*
- *Journal of Statistical Computation and Simulation*
- *Journal of Statistical Software*

REFERENCES

[1] A. C. Duffy, "Where do computational mathematics and computational statistics converge?" *WIREs Computational Statistics*, vol. 6, Sept./Oct. 2014, pp. 341–351.

[2] J. E. Gentle, "Courses in statistical computing and computational statistics," *The American Statistician*, vol. 58, no. 1, Feb. 2004, pp. 2–5.

[3] W. L. Martinez, "Computational statistics in MATLAB," *WIREs Computational Statistics*, vol. 3, Jan./Feb. 2011, pp. 69–74.

[4] M. N. O. Sadiku, M. Tembely, and S. M. Musa, "Computational statistics," *International Journal of Advanced Research in Computer Science and Software Engineering*, vol. 8, no. 7, July 2018, pp. 76–78.

[5] J. E. Gentle, *Computational Statistics*. New York: Springer, 2009.

[6] K. Lange, "Computational statistics and optimization theory at UCLA," *The American Statistician*, vol. 58, no. 1, Feb. 2004, pp. 9–11.

[7] W. L. Martinez and A. R. Martinez, *Computational Statistics Handbook with MATLAB*, 3rd ed. Boca Raton, FL: CRC Press, 2016.

[8] W. K. Härdle and Y. Mori (eds.), *Handbook of Computational Statistics: Concepts and Methods*, 2nd ed. New York: Springer, 2012.

[9] J. E. Gentle, G. H. Givens, and J. A. Hoeting, *Computational Statistics*, 2nd ed. Hoboken, NJ: John Wiley & Sons, 2013.

[10] W. Härdle, O. Okhrin, and Y. Okhrin, *Basic Elements of Computational Statistics*. Springer, 2017.

[11] J. E. Gentle, *Elements of Computational Statistics*. Springer, 2002.

CHAPTER 15

COMPUTATIONAL ECONOMICS

"In the new economy, information, education, and motivation are everything."

– William J. Clinton

15.1 INTRODUCTION

The increasing power of computers has given economic scientists new opportunities and vast potential. As far as computation is concerned, economics is undergoing the same transformation as physics, chemistry, social science, sociology, biology, and other hard sciences.

Computational economics (CE) is a marriage between computer science and traditional economics. In a sense, CE is a new programming methodology. CE solves problems that are difficult to study without the use of computers. For example, computational tools include software for carrying out various matrix operations and for solving systems of linear and nonlinear equations. Computational techniques have successfully been applied to solve problems in these areas.

A newly emerging branch of CE has come to be known as agent-based computational economics (ACE), the computational study of economies modeled as evolving systems of autonomous interacting agents. ACE allows us to model complex sets of relationships that cannot be explicitly modeled using traditional approaches. It is the computational study of economies modeled as evolving systems of autonomous interacting agents with learning capabilities. The economic agents can include consumers, producers, intermediaries, etc. ACE assumes that agents are heterogeneous and rational and that they interact with each other. It offers the possibility of modeling agents that learn and adapt to their environment [1].

Students working on CE acquire model development skills. These skills are the ability to conceptualize the science, engineering, and economics of a problem and to convert that understanding first into a mathematical model and then into a computational representation in a software system [2].

The recent advances in modeling tools have greatly expanded the possibility set for economists. This has led to the rapid emergence of computational economics as an independent branch of economics. Computational economics is a multidisciplinary field that explores the interaction of economics and computational systems. It has added a new dimension to microelectronics [3].

This chapter provides an introduction to computational economics. It begins with presenting some applications of computational economics. It addresses some challenges of computational economics. The last section concludes with comments.

15.2 APPLICATIONS

Although the tools and approaches may differ, the agendas of traditional economics and CE are complementary. CE modeling is a complement, not a substitute, for analytical modeling approaches. The

CE approach to economic problems is novel. It exploits new powerful computational tools, most notably object-oriented programming. These tools permit CE researchers to extend previous work on economic self-organization and evolution.

The application of CE addresses two key questions: whether a particular CE problem is solvable in principle and whether it is solvable in practice. Computational economics has been powerfully applied to a number of economic systems, and the most successful and attractive one is probably the agent-based financial market. CE tools have been used to handle economic problems such as cyclical growth, monopolist searching, adaptively learning duopoly, multiplier-accelerator dynamics based on the different behavior of investors, etc., using appropriate software such as MATLAB-SIMULINK, STELLA, VENSIM, SWARM, GEMODEL, NetLogo, Mathematica, and EXCEL [4].

CE tools have also been applied to forecast financial time series, estimate econometric parameters, model trade processes, replicate laboratory results with human subjects, simulate artificial stock markets and social processes, design public policies, simulate policy options, and develop worldwide models of some industries, etc. [5,6].

One of the areas in economics that requires high computing power is macroeconometric modeling with forward-looking variables because it involves very large systems of equations. Multicore processors, GPU computing, and MPI clusters have become available to economists for solving large problems that require high-performance computing [7].

15.3 CHALLENGES

It has been difficult for computational economics to gain acceptance as a tool for the analysis of economic models. There is little agreement on how to present computational results. There is no common core of methods. The combination of poor scholarship, poor grasp of basic computational methods, and sloppy standards combine to make computational economics look bad in the eyes of those aware of the problems [8]. CE requires interdisciplinary collaboration, but communication across disciplinary lines can be difficult.

Attempts by researchers to conduct parallel experiments with real and computational agents have raised a number of challenging issues. One challenge is that experiments run with human participants generally have to be kept short to avoid boredom among the participants [9].

15.4 CONCLUSION

Computational economics is a means of solving economic problems with the help of computing tools. The new directions in supercomputing are beneficial to computational economics. We are approaching an era where computing tools are sufficiently advanced and user-friendly that one does not have to be a specialist to use them effectively.

The field of CE is growing steadily, as evidenced by specific societies, journals, workgroups, and courses (even an M.Sc. degree) [10]. The need for computational economics courses in undergraduate and graduate programs is becoming increasingly apparent to economists.

For more information on computational economics, consult *Computational Economics* (the official journal of the Society for Computational Economics that came into being in 1994), the *Journal of Economic Dynamics and Control (JEDC)*, *ACM Transactions on Economics and Computation*, and the *International Journal of Computational Economics and Econometrics*. These are internationally competitive, peer-reviewed journals dedicated to research on CE.

REFERENCES

[1] A. Okasha and C. Johnson, "Agent-based computational economics: studying the effect of different levels of rationality on inflation and unemployment," *IEEE Symposium on Computational Intelligence for Financial Engineering*, March/April 2009.

[2] D. A. Kendrick, "Teaching computational economics to graduate students," *Computational Economics*, vol. 30, 2007, pp. 381–391.

[3] M. N. O. Sadiku, M. Tembely, and S. M. Musa, "Computational economics," *International Journal of Engineering Research*, vol. 6, no. 11, Nov. 2017, pp. 464–465.

[4] L. Andrasik, "Computational qualitative economics – using computational intelligence for advanced learning of economics in knowledge society," *The Journal of Pan-European*, vol. 5, no. 2, December 2015, pp. 1–15.

[5] P. Isasi, "Computational finance and economics technical committee," *IEEE Computational Intelligence Magazine*, May 2007, p. 73.

[6] D. A. Kendrick, "Research opportunities in computational economics," *Computational Economics*, vol. 6, 1993, pp. 257–314.

[7] B. Oancea, "Parallel computing in economics – an overview of software frameworks," *Challenges of the Knowledge Society*, vol. 1, no. 1, May 2014, pp. 1031–1043.

[8] K. L. Judd, "Computational economics and economic theory: substitutes or complements?" *Journal of Economic Dynamics and Control*, vol. 21, 1997, pp. 907–942.

[9] L. Tesfatsion, "Agent-based computational economics: modeling economies as complex adaptive systems," *Information Sciences*, vol. 149, 2003, pp. 263–269.

[10] U. Kaymak, "An MSc program in computational economics with a focus on computational intelligence," *IEEE Computational Intelligence Magazine*, May 2006, p. 41.

CHAPTER 16

COMPUTATIONAL FINANCE

"He who asks a question is a fool for five minutes; he who does not ask a question remains a fool forever."

– Chinese Proverb

16.1 INTRODUCTION

Rapid advances in computing hardware and algorithms have changed our society, particularly our financial markets. Never before have we had large amounts of financial data to analyze and the computer processing power to analyze them [1].

Financial institutions and financial markets became increasingly dependent on computers, and their productivity has improved steadily by the use of computers to manage databases and process transactions. Financial markets are complex and dynamic. As the market has grown, new branches of finance have emerged. A newly emerging field that combines mathematics, economics, and computation has become known as computational finance [2]. While traditional finance deals with actually making transactions that range from stock trades to corporate acquisitions, computational finance is more concerned with algorithms, modeling, and the computer software that powers most of the modern financial world.

The two major approaches used in CF are the partial differential equation (PDE) approach, which relies on finite difference (FD) methods, and the probabilistic approach, which is based on Monte Carlo (MC) simulation. Several numerical methods have been developed for both of the above approaches [3]. FD involves the simple discretization of differential equations. Monte Carlo methods are probabilistic techniques that employ random numbers to simulate stochastic behavior. They have great potential regarding speedup, fault tolerance, and scalability on a wide range of applications. They are important tools for approximating high-dimensional integrals in CF.

As CF developed, it came to rely on massive algorithms and "big data." Over the years, the field has expanded into other areas of finance, and the demand for CF practitioners has grown dramatically. One such area is agent-based computational finance, which emphasizes interactions and learning dynamics among heterogeneous traders, who consist of a very diverse set of types and behaviors [4]. With agent-based computational finance models, along with computer technology and artificial intelligence, it is possible to simulate the dynamic evolution of complex financial markets.

Computational finance is crucial to the security and welfare of any nation. It is becoming indispensable in many scientific investigations ranging from chemistry, physics, mathematics, aerospace, economics, and finance. Computational finance is an important aspect of modern commerce. It combines the power of computing and statistical analysis with the principles of finance and investment management [5].

This chapter serves as an introduction to computational finance. It begins with providing some applications of computational finance. It addresses the challenges of computational finance. The last section concludes with comments.

16.2 APPLICATIONS

CF is a field that combines different cultures. It relies on computer technology, computational intelligence, mathematical finance, and simulations. Financial engineering and algorithmic trading are perhaps two of the most computationally intensive parts of finance. The creation of a CF application usually involves two steps [6]:

- The creation of a numerical component using Visual C++ or Visual FORTRAN.
- The construction of the application framework using Microsoft languages such as Visual Basic.

CF is widely applied in financial economics, option pricing, large-scale investment trading, algorithmic stock trading, quantitative investing, and algorithmic investment management. It can be used to model the randomness of a stock's price. At some future times, the stock's price is modeled as a random variable with a normal distribution centered around the current price [7]. Some financial codes or software are written in C, C++, or MATLAB.

16.3 CHALLENGES

It has not been easy for computational finance to gain wide acceptance as a tool for analyzing and modeling financial problems. Financial institutions often lack research budgets compared to other industries because they do not regard finance as science. Computational finance is needed to deal with the complex and dynamic marketplace. Today, there is no repository with data that researchers can use to build predictive market models [8].

With the latest development in computer architectures, we are faced with the exascale computing challenge. The progress in the high-performance computing environment in recent years has led to large-scale machines at the petaflop level [9].

Besides computational complexity, challenges also come from cognitive reasoning. What is being questioned is how optimal human beings are. Some of the resources available to an agent are difficult to quantify.

Another major challenge to CF is the inadequacy of qualitative risk infrastructure within global financial institutions.

16.4 CONCLUSION

Computational finance has been gaining attention from the business community due to the increasing availability of financial information for analysis and positive changes in computer processing power. It is a growing and diverse field. CF professionals come from varied academic backgrounds such as computer science, information systems, business administration, and finance. Most of these typically studied either computer science or finance at the undergraduate level.

Graduates who specialize in CF will be qualified to work in pricing financial risk, in credit risk and their derivatives, and in cutting-edge institutions. They should be well grounded in data-intensive computing, visualization, and simulation because one wrong algorithmic program could result in financial disaster for individuals, retirement firms, stocks, corporations, and many other stakeholders.

REFERENCES

[1] E. P. K. Tsang and S. Martinez-Jaramillo, "Computational finance," *IEEE Computational Intelligence Society Newsletter*, August 2004, pp. 3–8.

[2] K. Northover and A. W. Lo, "Computational finance," *Computing in Science & Engineering*, November/December 1999, pp. 22–23.

[3] J. R. Varma and V. Virmani, "Computational finance using QuantLib-Python," *Computing in Science & Engineering*, March/April 2016, pp. 78–88.

[4] B. LeBaron, "Agent-based computational finance: suggested readings and early research," *Journal of Economic Dynamics & Control*, vol. 24, 2000, pp. 679–702.

[5] M. N. O. Sadiku, S. M. Musa, and O. S. Musa, "Computational finance," *International Journal of Trend in Research and Development*, vol. 4, no. 5, Sept./Oct. 2017, pp. 375–376.

[6] G. Levy, *Computational Finance: Numerical Methods for Pricing Financial Instruments*. Burlington, MA: Elsevier, 2004, p. 5.

[7] M. G. Hilgers, "Computational finance tool," *IEEE Potentials*, Dec. 2000/Jan. 2001, pp. 8–10. [8] R. Olsen, "Computational finance as a driver of economics: a research agenda for financial studies," *IEEE Computational Intelligence Magazine*, November 2008, pp. 35–38.

[9] V. N. Alexandrov, C. G. Martel, and J. Strabburg, "Monte Carlo scalable algorithms for computational finance," *Procedia Computer Science*, vol. 4, 2011, pp. 1708–1715.

CHAPTER 17

COMPUTATIONAL HUMANITIES

"Be certain that you do not die without having done something wonderful for humanity."

– Maya Angelou

17.1 INTRODUCTION

Computational thinking is an intellectual revolution that is influencing research in nearly all disciplines, both in the sciences and the humanities. It provides a new way of asking research questions and describing problems. It is a kind of analytical thinking and approach that cuts across many disciplines and funding agencies [1]. Computational thinking is bound to influence everyone in our society, including children. This implies that computational thinking will touch everyone directly or indirectly [2].

An increasing interest in the use of computational thinking and techniques is something that the humanities hold in common with other fields. The use of computers and the Internet has expanded enormously in different humanities disciplines over the past years. The computer provides access to data and improves the opportunities for data analysis and visualization. Much of the research funding these days has computational aspects [3,4].

Computational humanities is at the intersection of computing technologies and the disciplines of the humanities. Research in this field has steadily increased over the past years. Computational tools supporting textual search, large database analysis, data mining, network mapping, and natural language processing are employed by humanities researchers. This opens up new realms for analysis and understanding [5].

This chapter provides an introduction to computational humanities. It begins with describing the humanities. It defines computational humanities. It addresses challenges of computational humanities. The last section concludes with comments.

17.2 CONCEPT OF HUMANITIES

The humanities cover what we commonly call the liberal arts: art, literature, history, anthropology, philosophy, music, media studies, archaeology, geography, and language studies. Our society would be poorer without the humanities helping us to understand what it means to be human and humane in today's complex world. Technology is making the humanities more engaging and more accessible.

17.3 DEFINING COMPUTATIONAL HUMANITIES

Computational humanities (CH) has been practiced by an international community of scholars since the late 1940s. It is still an emerging discipline with its momentum arising from the growing application of information technology [6]. It refers to research into the humanities through advanced computing technologies. It involves using computers as tools for modeling and analyzing humanities data [7].

It is a young and exploratory area of computationally based research that meets the grand challenges of our time. It is a necessary approach for researchers who wish to investigate the numerous human activities using a computer. The key players in computational humanities include Google, Facebook, YouTube, and other companies that analyze social media signals (blogs, Twitter, etc.).

17.4 CHALLENGES

One of the problems most humanities scholars face is lack of direct access to events, phenomena, and sites of interest for their research. Virtual heritage is an excellent tool that helps many humanities scholars learn about previous worlds. Virtual reality users are strongly affected by the environment and its characters. These tools open many possibilities for research in the humanities by providing virtual access to material and applying interaction methods that mimic real-world actions [8].

Another challenge in computational humanities is demystifying the technology for non-technologists. Computer scientists and humanities scholars need to communicate effectively as they work together.

While computational humanities is provocative and important, it remains marginal to mainstream scholarship. Humanities scholars are noted for their tendency to work alone and are rewarded for originality.

17.5 CONCLUSION

The use of computational techniques in the study of the humanities is still young and exploratory. Responding to the computational transformation of the humanities will take a while. CH creates opportunities for interdisciplinary collaboration between humanities scholars and computer scientists. Some universities have started to offer courses in computational humanities. These courses basically teach and train humanities students in computing [9,10].

REFERENCES

[1] A. Bundy, "Computational thinking is pervasive," *Journal of Scientific and Practical Computing Noted Reviews*, vol. 1, no. 2, 2007, pp. 67–69.

[2] J. M. Wing, "Computational thinking and thinking about computing," *Philosophical Transactions of the Royal Society A*, vol. 366, 2008, pp. 3717–3725.

[3] M. Katzen, "The application of computers in the humanities: a view from Britain," *Information Processing & Management*, vol. 22, no. 1, 1986, pp. 259–267.

[4] J. Nerbonne et al., "Panel discussion on computing and the humanities," *International Journal of Humanities and Arts Computing*, vol. 2, no. 1–2, 2008, pp. 19–37.

[5] M. N. O. Sadiku, N. K. Ampah, and S. M. Musa, "Computational humanities," *International Journal of Advanced Research in Computer Science and Software Engineering*, vol. 8, no. 6, June 2018, pp. 45–46.

[6] W. Kaltenbrunner, "Decomposition as practice and process: creating boundary objects in computational humanities," *Interdisciplinary Science Reviews*, vol. 39, no. 2, June 2014, pp. 143–161.

[7] M. Terras, J. Nyhan, and E. Vanhoutte (eds.), *Defining Digital Humanities: A Reader*. Surrey, UK: Ashgate Publishing Limited, 2013.

[8] C. Cruz-Neira, "Computational humanities: the new challenge for VR," *IEEE Computer Graphics and Applications*, May/June 2003, pp. 10–13.

[9] J. Bunde and D. Engel, "Computing in the humanities: an interdisciplinary partnership in undergraduate education," *Journal of Archival Organization*, vol. 8, 2010, pp. 149–159.

[10] N. M. Ide, "Computers and the humanities courses: philosophical bases and approach," *Computers and the Humanities*, vol. 21, 1987, p. 209.

CHAPTER 18

COMPUTATIONAL SOCIOLOGY

"Success doesn't discriminate. It's an equal opportunity employer – available to everyone willing to pay the price."

– Anonymous

18.1 INTRODUCTION

Sociology is the study of the fundamental laws of social relations, institutions, organizations, etc. It deals with explaining and predicting social behavior. It involves explaining how multiple factors interact in complex ways to affect social behaviors and in explaining the dynamics by which social groups, organizations, societies, and cultures evolve [1]. It equips us with the capacity to explain important elements of social life.

Technological innovations have led to major transformations in science and social sciences. The familiar two-component model of any science now includes the third component—computation. For instance, we now have theoretical physics, experimental physics, and computational physics. Computing and information processing have transformed sociology. Computational sociology utilizes modern computer science to advance sociology [2]. It has a long tradition that goes back to the 1960s.

This chapter begins with explaining computational sociology. It describes computer simulations and agent-based modeling. It addresses some challenges of computational sociology. The last section concludes with comments.

18.2 COMPUTATIONAL SOCIOLOGY

Computational sociology is an emerging area in sociology that applies computational tools to solve and analyze social problems. It uses computer algorithms, computer simulations, and artificial intelligence to model social phenomena. The most recent wave of computational sociology, rather than employing simulations, uses network analysis, statistical techniques, and agent-based modeling to analyze large-scale computer databases of behavioral data [3].

Computational sociology is a branch of sociology where advances in computational techniques (e.g., simulation, emulation, artificial intelligence, expert systems) are merged with sociological reasoning. Computation has been used in sociology to solve complex existing problems [4].

18.3 COMPUTER SIMULATIONS

In a sense, simulation can be considered a substitute for experimentation. It can help us investigate some situations that cannot be investigated through experiments. Computer simulations represent real-world conditions using a computer program that mimics the processes of a system. Since a computer program is more precise than a written description, computer simulation allows easier and more controlled manipulation of system variables [5].

Recent advances in both hardware and software have created new interest in using simulation as a modeling tool. Simulation allows us to analyze complex systems that are impossible to study using traditional methods. Computer simulations investigate how social processes unfold and how interaction structures influence social outcomes. Powerful computer models have become tools for solving many problems in science, engineering, social science, and business [6].

Researchers and sociologists can use simulation to generate processes. Different simulation techniques have been developed: system dynamics, multi-agent systems, cellular automata, and genetic algorithms. Artificial agents and cellular automata are interesting tools in simulation. Artificial agents can be made to generate and respond to commands, perform tasks, and answer questions. Cellular automata are a particular kind of multi-agent system [7].

18.4 AGENT-BASED MODELING

Computational sociology has traditionally used computer simulation models to analyze social problems. A new wave in computational sociology is agent-based modeling (ABM). Agents are computer programs or codes which are executed independently within a simulated environment. ABM assumes that agents are autonomous, interdependent, follow simple rules, are adaptive, and are backward-looking. ABMs are most useful in modeling processes that lack central coordination [8]. They should be a standard technique for every social scientist.

Squazzoni's book on *Agent-Based Computational Sociology* provides an introduction to ABM from the perspective of sociological theory [9].

18.5 CHALLENGES

A major challenge of computer simulation in sociology is the search for tools that are able to define the connection between the virtual world and the empirical world. Determining the validity of a computer simulation model can be a difficult undertaking.

Another challenge in computational sociology is demystifying the technology for non-technologists. Computer scientists and sociologists need to communicate effectively as they work together. To move the field forward, all sociology departments should be teaching the computer programming skills necessary to process and analyze big data, and computer scientists who are analyzing social data should also be taught social science.

While computational sociology is provocative and important, it remains marginal to mainstream scholarship. Sociology has lagged behind other social sciences in appreciating and embracing this emerging methodology [8].

18.6 CONCLUSION

Computational sociology involves using computing techniques, such as computer simulation and agent-based modeling, to analyze social phenomena and to understand, explain, and predict social behavior. It provides an opportunity to integrate traditionally disparate approaches within sociology and transforms sociology in the 21st century. Research in this interdisciplinary area grows out of work in many scientific disciplines including sociology, psychology, organization theory, artificial intelligence, computing, and information processing.

For examples of research in this area, see the *Journal of Artificial Societies and Social Simulation* (http://jasss.soc.surrey.ac.uk/).

REFERENCES

[1] K. M. Carley, "Computational approaches to sociological theorizing," in J. Turner (ed.), *Handbook of Sociological Theory*. New York, NY: Kluwer Academic/Plenum Publishers, 2001, ch. 4, pp. 69–84.

[2] N. P. Hummon and T. J. Fararo, "The emergence of computational sociology," *Journal of Mathematical Sociology*, vol. 20, no. 2–3, 1995, pp. 79–87.

[3] "Computational sociology," *Wikipedia, the free encyclopedia*. Available: https://en.wikipedia.org/wiki/Computational_sociology

[4] M. N. O. Sadiku, S. M. Musa, and S. Alam, "Computational sociology," *International Journal of Engineering Research and Allied Sciences*, vol. 2, no. 5, May 2017, pp. 4–5.

[5] "Computational sociology research paper starter."

Available:https://www.enotes.com/research-starters/computational-sociology

[6] S. Bankes, R. Lempert, and S. Popper, "Making computational social science effective: epistemology, methodology, and technology," *Social Science Computer Review*, vol. 20, no. 4, Winter 2002, pp. 377–388.

[7] S. Moretti, "Computer simulation in sociology: what contribution?" *Social Science Computer Review*, vol. 20, no. 1, Spring 2002, pp. 43–57.

[8] M. W. Macy and R. Willer, "From factors to actors: computational sociology and agent-based modeling," *Annual Review of Sociology*, vol. 28, 2002, pp. 143–166.

[9] F. Squazzoni, *Agent-Based Computational Sociology*. Chichester, West Sussex, UK: John Wiley & Sons, 2012.

CHAPTER 19

COMPUTATIONAL LINGUISTICS

"Time is:

Too slow for those who wait

Too swift for those who fear

Too long for those who grieve

Too short for those who rejoice

But for those who love, time is not.

— Henry Van Dyke

19.1 INTRODUCTION

Everywhere, every day, everybody uses language. There is no human society that does not employ a language. Computational linguistics (CL) is based on the idea that machines can be programmed to understand, learn, or output languages. It is often linked with natural language processing (NLP) and natural language generation (NLG), which are subsets of it. NLP enables a computer program to understand human language as it is written or spoken. The NLP engine is programmed to interpret written commands naturally using simple rules. NLG refers to the use of computers to generate language. Computers that are linguistically competent help facilitate human interaction with machines and software.

Linguistics is concerned with rules that are followed by languages as systems. Computational linguistics combines the power of machine learning with human language. As a subfield of linguistics, CL focuses on the computational description of rules that languages follow. It powers anything in a machine or device that involves language—speaking, writing, reading, and listening. It is often linked with NLP, which uses computers to identify structures in natural language. The boundary between NLP and CL is not always clear-cut [1].

This chapter is a primer on computational linguistics. It begins by explaining computational linguistics, then explores how to become a computational linguist, provides applications, highlights benefits and challenges, and concludes with final comments.

19.2 COMPUTATIONAL LINGUISTICS

Computational linguistics first emerged in the 1950s with machine translation, when the United States military attempted to develop programs to automatically translate Russian text into English and Chinese text into English. The idea was that computers could make systematic calculations faster and more accurately than people. Since its inception, CL has gone through several iterations. Research on CL has benefited greatly from work in artificial intelligence.

It is the process of deciphering what customers are asking and prompting AI to deliver accurate responses to their questions based on internal data. Modern CL relies on tools such as AI, machine learning, deep learning, and cognitive computing.

Computational linguistics is an interdisciplinary field that applies computer science (and the use of algorithms) to analyze and comprehend written and spoken language. As shown in Figure 19.1,

CL combines linguistics, computer science, artificial intelligence, mathematics, psychology, engineering, cognitive science, and philosophy [2].

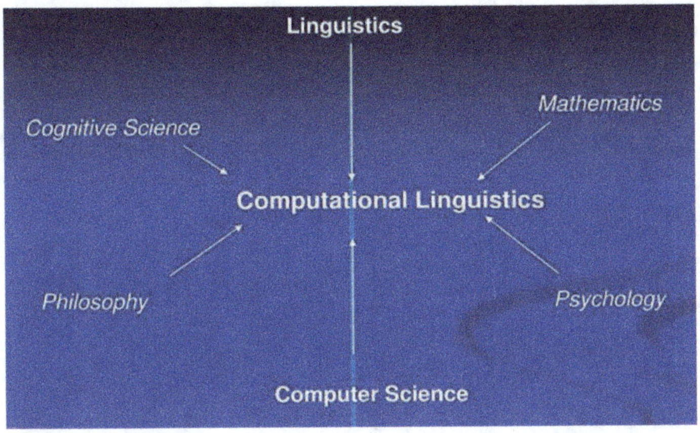

Figure 19.1 - Computational linguistics as an interdisciplinary field [2].

19.3 BECOMING A COMPUTATIONAL LINGUIST

Computational linguists transform unstructured and structured data into something useful. To start the journey of becoming a computational linguist, one typically needs a degree in computer science, computer engineering, linguistics, or a related field. This could be a bachelor's, master's, doctoral, or associate degree.

It is recommended to first build computer science skills (coding, data structures, databases, data visualization, and machine learning) before studying linguistics. To program the algorithms used in CL, learning a programming language is essential. Python is a good option because it is widely used. Students should also be able to design and create applications for retrieving, processing, and visualizing data. Developing skills in math and statistics is also valuable.

Once comfortable with the necessary skills and knowledge, one can apply for positions in the field. Unfortunately, most opportunities are concentrated in large technology companies such as Amazon, Apple, and Grammarly [3].

Common business goals of CL include [4]:

- Creating grammatical and semantic frameworks for characterizing languages.
- Translating text from one language to another.
- Offering text and information retrieval for specific topics.
- Analyzing text or spoken language for context, sentiment, or affective qualities.
- Answering questions, including those requiring inference and descriptive responses.
- Summarizing text.
- Building dialogue agents capable of completing tasks such as purchases, trip planning, or scheduling.
- Creating chatbots capable of passing the Turing Test.
- Exploring the statistical and structural elements of language to understand learning and processing.

19.4 APPLICATIONS OF COMPUTATIONAL LINGUISTICS

CL has many real-world applications, including [3,5]:

- **Machine translation:** Using AI to translate between languages (e.g., Google Translate).
- **Chatbots:** Programs that simulate human conversation for customer service or entertainment. Early examples trace back to Weizenbaum's *ELIZA*.
- **Knowledge extraction:** Creating structured knowledge from text sources (e.g., Wikipedia).
- **Natural language interfaces:** Tools that let users interact with devices using speech (e.g., Siri, Alexa).
- **Sentiment analysis:** Identifying emotional tone in text or speech. Applications include marketing, political analysis, and social network studies. Grammarly is one example.
- **Text mining:** Extracting useful information from large volumes of unstructured data.

19.5 BENEFITS

Computational linguistics studies the computational processing, understanding, and generation of human languages. Work in this field, strengthened by advances in computing power, is motivated both by scientific goals (explaining linguistic phenomena computationally) and practical goals (improving interaction with machines).

Since much human knowledge is expressed in language, CL supports progress in customer service, research, and AI. It also provides insights into human thinking and intelligence.

Robots have been used to test linguistic theories and are increasingly equipped with capabilities such as web services, question answering, tutoring, and chatbots. Public interest in intelligent robots—given their applications in medicine, education, industry, eldercare, entertainment, agriculture, military missions, and space exploration—will continue to drive progress in robotic intelligence and linguistic competence [5].

19.6 CHALLENGES

AI leadership has recently become a two-horse race between China and the U.S. The pressure to publish results is intense, leading to a focus on incremental improvements rather than deep insight. Research priorities vary across regions: Europe emphasizes inclusiveness and community, while the U.S. pursues disruption, and China emphasizes bold initiatives.

Despite relatively strong funding in the U.S., Europe's research investment remains smaller compared to other regions. In China, industrial efforts are aggressive and milestone-driven. The U.S. is urged to increase investment to compete [6].

Language itself is complex. CL often treats language as a closed system, and challenges such as data privacy remain significant. Privacy concerns are particularly sensitive in Europe but less emphasized in Asia. Translation quality, while improving, still suffers from errors, though often sufficient for general comprehension.

19.7 CONCLUSION

Computational linguistics is now an active sub-discipline within applied linguistics and data science. It powers technologies such as chatbots and search engines. Applications range from basic pattern recognition to advanced systems capable of meaningful comprehension and communication.

At Amazon, computational linguists and engineers contribute to Alexa. At Apple, they help build Siri.

It has been demonstrated that languages can be learned incrementally as memory and attention span improve. Researchers have even created systems capable of predicting the future evolution of languages and analyzing their historical development [7].

For more details, see [8–32] and the following journals:

- *Computational Linguistics*
- *International Journal of Computational Linguistics*

REFERENCES

[1] M. N. O. Sadiku, C. M. M. Kotteti, and J. O. Sadiku, "Computational linguistics," *International Journal of Advances in Scientific Research and Engineering*, vol. 10, no. 1, January 2024, pp. 1–6.

[2] Yahoo Images, "Images for computational linguistics," https://images.search.yahoo.com/yhs/search#id=14&iurl=https%3A%2F%2Fimage2.slideserve.com%2F5312589%2Fslide9-1.jpg&action=click

[3] "What is computational linguistics? Insights and career guide," Coursera, November 2023

https://www.coursera.org/articles/computational-linguistics

[4] K. Yasar, A. S. Gillis, and C. Bernstein, "Computational linguistics (CL)," *TechTarget*.

https://www.techtarget.com/searchenterpriseai/definition/computational-linguistics-CL

[5] "Computational linguistics," *Stanford Encyclopedia of Philosophy*, February 2014.

https://plato.stanford.edu/entries/computational-linguistics/

[6] K. Church and M. Liberman, "The future of computational linguistics: On beyond alchemy," *Frontiers of Artificial Intelligence*, vol. 4, April 2021.

[7] "Computational linguistics," *Wikipedia, the free encyclopedia*. https://en.wikipedia.org/wiki/Computational_linguistics

[8] A. Przepiórkowski et al. (eds.), *Computational Linguistics: Application*. Springer, 2012.

[9] R. Grishman, *Computational Linguistics: An Introduction*. Cambridge University Press, 1986.

[10] B. McGillivray, *Methods in Latin Computational Linguistics*. Paris: Brill, 2013.

[11] G. Ferrari, *State of the Art in Computational Linguistics*. n.a., 2003.

[12] A. Gliozzo and C. Strapparava, *Semantic Domains in Computational Linguistics*. Springer Science & Business Media, 2009.

[13] F. Lamarche, A. Lecomte, and G. Perrier (eds.), *Logical Aspects of Computational Linguistics*. Springer, 1999.

[14] C. Souter and E. Atwell (eds.), *Corpus-based Computational Linguistics*. Rodopi, 1993.

[15] C. L. Paris, W. R. Swartout, and W. C. Mann (eds.), *Natural Language Generation in Artificial Intelligence and Computational Linguistics*. Springer Science & Business Media, 2013.

[16] B. Srinivasa-Desikan, *Natural Language Processing and Computational Linguistics: A Practical Guide to Text Analysis with Python, Gensim, spaCy, and Keras*. Packt Publishing, 2018.

[17] J. Heinz et al., *Grammatical Inference for Computational Linguistics*. Morgan & Claypool, 2016.

[18] M. Z. Kurdi, *Natural Language Processing and Computational Linguistics: Speech, Morphology and Syntax*, vol. 1. John Wiley & Sons, 2016.

[19] M. Z. Kurdi, *Natural Language Processing and Computational Linguistics 2: Semantics, Discourse and Applications*, vol. 2. John Wiley & Sons, 2017.

[20] G. Hirst, *Views of Text Meaning in Computational Linguistics: Past, Present, and Future*. n.a., 2007.

[21] A. Zampolli, N. Calzolari, and M. Palmer (eds.), *Current Issues in Computational Linguistics: In Honour of Don Walker*. Springer, 1994.

[22] G. Sidorov, *Syntactic n-grams in Computational Linguistics*. Cham, Switzerland: Springer International Publishing, 2019.

[23] D. Nouvel, M. Ehrmann, and S. Rosset, *Named Entities for Computational Linguistics*. John Wiley & Sons, 2016.

[24] R. Mitkov (ed.), *The Oxford Handbook of Computational Linguistics*. 2nd ed. Oxford University Press, 2014.

[25] A. Clark, C. Fox, and S. Lappin (eds.), *The Handbook of Computational Linguistics and Natural Language Processing*. Blackwell Publishing, 2010.

[26] *Computational Linguistics: Concepts, Methodologies, Tools, and Applications*. Information Science Reference, 2014.

[27] C. F. Alexander and S. Lappin (eds.), *The Handbook of Computational Linguistics and Natural Language Processing*. John Wiley & Sons, 2012.

[28] R. Grishman, *Computational Linguistics: An Introduction*. Cambridge University Press, 1986.

[29] R. Hausser, *Foundations of Computational Linguistics: Human–Computer Communication in Natural Language*. 3rd ed. Springer-Verlag, 2001.

[30] N. Dershowitz and E. Nissan (eds.), *Language, Culture, Computation: Computational Linguistics*. Springer, 2014.

[31] S. Pogodalla, *Logical Aspects of Computational Linguistics*. Springer, 2011.

[32] S. Abney, *Semisupervised Learning for Computational Linguistics*. Boca Raton, FL: CRC Press, 2007.

CHAPTER 20

COMPUTATIONAL MEDICINE

"Your food is supposed to be your medicine and your medicine is supposed to be your food."

– African Proverb

20.1 INTRODUCTION

Computational modeling has been tremendously successful in engineering. A great challenge is to extend the success of computational modeling to fields outside traditional engineering, such as medicine. Computational medicine (CM) is a fast-growing method of using computer models to investigate how disease develops. With the assistance of CM, research in the field of medicine has gained tremendous benefits and expansion over the past few decades. Since biological systems are inherently complex, computational models are needed to understand their function in health and disease. In the new era of data-driven personalized medicine, we will rely more on the help of computational analysis [1].

The dramatic advances in software and hardware development during the past half-century suggest that our computational efforts in the next half-century will supersede all imagination. By applying digital tools, researchers have begun to build models that can unravel complex medical mysteries. The field of computational medicine is exciting and important [2].

This chapter provides an introduction to computational medicine. It begins with explaining computational medicine. It gives some examples of computational medicine. It addresses the challenges of computational medicine. The last section concludes with comments.

20.2 COMPUTATIONAL MEDICINE

Computational medicine is an emerging discipline that harnesses the power of computers to solve real problems in medicine and clinical research. As a scientific discipline, computational medicine encompasses all aspects of applying computers and computing models to support medical research in health care services. In this chapter, we will see how computing can address issues facing health sciences.

20.3 COMPUTATION EXAMPLES

CM has been successfully applied to cancer, diabetes, and heart disease. Winslow, the first author of the Science Translational Medicine overview, describes examples of computational medicine [3]:

- Advanced mathematical models allow researchers to understand how networks of molecules are implicated in cancer and then use this knowledge to predict which patients are at risk of developing the disease.
- Computational physiological medicine uses computer models to look at how biological systems change over time from a healthy to an unhealthy state.
- Computational anatomy uses medical images to detect changes, for example, in the shape of various structures in the brain.

- Computational models of electrical activity in the heart are on their way to being used to guide doctors in preventing sudden cardiac death and in diagnosing and treating those at risk for it.

To solve a sample computation of a bioelectric field problem may involve the following steps [4]:

1. Construct, manipulate, and display large-scale, three-dimensional geometric models.
2. Develop a three-dimensional, finite element program for elliptic partial differential equations with general boundary conditions and source terms.
3. Apply global and local regularization and solve the system of equations.
4. Use visualization tools for displaying the results.

Visualization enables researchers to observe the results of their computation. NMR, CAT, and PET scanners are now routinely used in most hospitals. They allow the physician to simulate surgery before carrying it out on the actual patient [5]. These days, the four steps mentioned above are routinely implemented using finite element–based software packages such as COMSOL and High Frequency Structure Simulator (HFSS). These packages put powerful tools and techniques, previously available only to full-time theorists, into the hands of health-care professionals [6].

20.4 CHALLENGES WITH CM

With the advent of powerful computing tools, researchers have been able to understand the intricate dynamics involved in diseases. However, these tools must often be checked with real-world data and adjusted accordingly [7].

A major challenge of computer simulation in medicine is the search for tools that are able to define the connection between the virtual world and the empirical world. Determining the validity of a computer simulation model can be a difficult undertaking.

Another challenge in computational medicine is demystifying the technology for nontechnologists. Computer scientists and medical scholars need to communicate effectively as they work together.

While computational medicine is provocative and important, it remains marginal to mainstream scholarship.

20.5 CONCLUSION

Computational medicine has greatly helped in the analysis of biological information. Computational tools are now in the hands of doctors who treat patients with all kinds of illnesses. They should be multilingual and user-friendly so they can be accessed by experts in different nations.

The Institute for Computational Medicine at Johns Hopkins University offers a multidisciplinary undergraduate minor in computational medicine. Imperial College London is launching a 10-week module for undergraduate medical students learning computational medicine. Computational medicine will provide a quantitative approach to our understanding, detecting, and treating diseases.

REFERENCES

[1] Y. Zhang et al., "Opportunities for computational techniques for multi-omics integrated personalized medicine," *Tsinghua Science and Technology*, vol. 19, no. 6, December 2014, pp. 545–558.

[2] M. N. O. Sadiku, M. Tembely, and S. M. Musa, "Computational medicine," *International Journal of Advanced Research in Computer Science and Software Engineering*, vol. 7, no. 4, April 2017, pp. 281–282.

[3] R. Winslow, "Computational medicine enhances way doctors detect, treat disease," Johns Hopkins University, November 2012. [Online]. Available:

http://releases.jhu.edu/2012/11/01/computational-medicine/

[4] C. R. Johnson, R. S. Macleod, and M. A. Matheson, "Computational medicine: bioelectric field problems," *Computer*, vol. 26, no. 10, October 1993, pp. 59–67.

[5] M. Witten, "Computational medicine," *IEEE Potentials*, October 1991, pp. 9–13.

[6] M. N. O. Sadiku, *Elements of Electromagnetics*, 6th ed. New York, NY: Oxford University Press, 2015, p. 732.

[7] K. Harmon, "How computational models are improving medicine [video]," *Scientific American*, November 2012. [Online]. Available: https://blogs.scientificamerican.com/observations/how-computational-models-are-improving-medicine-video/

INDEX

www.ingramcontent.com/pod-product-compliance
Lightning Source LLC
LaVergne TN
LVHW011514200926
848484LV00001B/38